...h longest established

Rely on Thomas Cook as your
travelling companion on your next trip
and benefit from our unique heritage.

Thomas Cook **pocket** guides

HELSINKI

Thomas
Cook

Your travelling companion since 1873

Written by Barbara Radcliffe Rogers & Stillman Rogers
Updated by Veera Julkunen

Published by Thomas Cook Publishing
A division of Thomas Cook Tour Operations Limited
Company registration No: 3772199 England
The Thomas Cook Business Park, 9 Coningsby Road
Peterborough PE3 8SB, United Kingdom
Email: books@thomascook.com, Tel: +44 (0)1733 416477
www.thomascookpublishing.com

Produced by The Content Works Ltd
Aston Court, Kingsmead Business Park, Frederick Place
High Wycombe, Bucks HP11 1LA
www.thecontentworks.com

Series design based on an original concept by Studio 183 Limited

ISBN: 978-1-84848-291-3

First edition © 2006 Thomas Cook Publishing
This third edition © 2010 Thomas Cook Publishing
Text © Thomas Cook Publishing
Maps © Thomas Cook Publishing/PCGraphics (UK) Limited
Transport map © Communicarta Limited

Project Editor: Kelly Anne Pipes
Production/DTP: Steven Collins

Printed and bound in Spain by GraphyCems

Cover photography (Double-headed eagle, Kauppatori) © David Noble
Photography/Alamy

All rights reserved. No part of this publication may be reproduced, stored in a retrieval
system or transmitted, in any form or any means, electronic, mechanical, recording
or otherwise, in any part of the world, without prior permission of the publisher.
Requests for permission should be made to the publisher at the above address.

Although every care has been taken in compiling this publication, and the contents
are believed to be correct at the time of printing, Thomas Cook Tour Operations
Limited cannot accept any responsibility for errors or omission, however caused,
or for changes in details given in the guidebook, or for the consequences of any
reliance on the information provided. Descriptions and assessments are based on
the author's views and experiences when writing and do not necessarily represent
those of Thomas Cook Tour Operations Limited.

CONTENTS

INTRODUCING HELSINKI
Introduction.................................6
When to go...................................8
The National Romantics..............14
History.......................................16
Lifestyle.....................................18
Culture.......................................20

MAKING THE MOST OF HELSINKI
Shopping.....................................24
Eating & drinking........................26
Entertainment & nightlife...........30
Sport & relaxation......................34
Accommodation..........................36
The best of Helsinki....................42
Suggested itineraries..................44
Something for nothing................46
When it rains..............................48
On arrival...................................50

THE CITY OF HELSINKI
Esplanadi & the Harbour.............62
Western & northern
    Helsinki.................................86
The islands & outskirts..............106

OUT OF TOWN TRIPS
Porvoo......................................124
Turku..130

PRACTICAL INFORMATION
Directory...................................142
Emergencies..............................154

INDEX.................................156

MAPS
Helsinki......................................52
Helsinki transport map...............56
Esplanadi & the Harbour............63
Western & northern
    Helsinki.................................87
The islands & outskirts..............107
Around Helsinki.........................126

SYMBOLS KEY

The following symbols are used throughout this book:

ⓐ address ⓣ telephone ⓦ website address ⓔ email
ⓛ opening times ⓝ public transport connections ⓘ important

The following symbols are used on the maps:

ⓘ	information office	▨	points of interest
✈	airport	○	city
✚	hospital	○	large town
⛨	police station	○	small town
⊟	bus station	═	motorway
⊟	railway station	—	main road
Ⓜ	metro		minor road
✝	cathedral	—	railway
❶	numbers denote featured cafés & restaurants		

Hotels and restaurants are graded by approximate price as follows:
£ budget price ££ mid-range price £££ expensive

▶ *Rooftops view towards the Lutheran Cathedral*

INTRODUCING
Helsinki

Introduction

Helsinki's beauty hits you right between the eyes, not least because some of the greatest architects in the world designed its buildings, which are set amid parks and against watery backdrops. Its beauty deserves a closer look, whether it's into shop windows filled with smart Finnish design or inside buildings whose interiors match their stunning outside views. But Helsinki is much more than just another pretty face. It is a friendly, exciting, warm-hearted place filled with people whose wry attitude to life will make you laugh and whose nightlife will keep you dancing into the early hours of the morning. It is blessed by almost round-the-clock sunlight in the summer, when no-one ever seems to sleep, and a population that knows how to make the most of the long snowy winter. Join them on skis or snowshoes in the parks, on paths that glitter with lights reflecting in the snow, or skate across the frozen bay of Töölönlahti. Warming up is no problem: take a sauna (you can choose from traditional wood-fired or modern state-of-the-art spas), knock back a steaming cup of *glögi* (mulled wine), go to a jazz club to hear authentic Dixieland, or dance to whatever moves your shoes.

Helsinki seems to be always on the move, with a star-studded line-up of festivals celebrating everything from samba and world cultures to heavy metal and Gay Pride. Downtown streets rock at night, and the buzz comes from people having a good time, not trying to impress one another with their dress or their oh-so-cool attitudes. Maybe that's because they know – and know the world knows it, too – that they have a great deal to declare at the customs of fashionable good taste. Whatever's new, you'll see it here first, not because the Finns have rushed out to buy it, but because they have designed it themselves. Here, you'll sense that you are on the cutting edge, whether you're dining on the latest plates from Arabia, drinking out of the newest Iittala stemware, lounging in an Alvar Aalto chair or geeking out on your smartphone.

It's hard not to have a good time in Helsinki, especially when things heat up at night. Perhaps that's the city's biggest surprise – and it's certainly what makes it so much fun to visit.

⬤ *World-famous Finnish design*

When to go

SEASONS & CLIMATE

With northern perversity, Helsinki's climate brings the most rain during the warm summer months, and the best chance of sparkling sunny days in winter. Summer temperatures hover around 20°C (68°F) and winter averages around -4°C (25°F). The winters can be cold sometimes, with temperatures dropping as low as -20°C (-4°F). The most popular months to visit are between May and September, but the city is pleasant year-round, as long as you remember a raincoat in the summer and warm coat (and boots) in the winter.

Snow is frequent in winter, but rarely deep in the city centre, often melting away quickly. In the rural areas there is permanent snow for the whole winter and it can get deep, especially in northern Finland. Light reflecting on the snow makes the city lighter during the short mid-winter days from November to January, when the sun doesn't rise until late morning and sets by around three in the afternoon.

● *Heavy snowfalls in the park don't deter Helsinki walkers*

ANNUAL EVENTS

January

Art Meets Ice (International Ice Sculpture Competition) Competitors from around the world gather at Korkeasaari Zoo (see page 109) to carve ice into artistic forms, which are left on display until they melt. Advance booking is recommended (tickets: Ⓦ www.lippupalvelu.fi). Ⓦ www.korkeasaari.fi/artmeetsice

DocPoint This documentary festival at the end of January features films not only from Finland and the Baltic states but also from around the world. ⓐ Fredrikinkatu 23 ⓣ 09 672 472 Ⓦ www.docpoint.info

March

Kirkko Soikoon (Church Music Festival) Churches honour Finnish and other Scandinavian religious music genres with orchestral, choral and solo performances in beautiful, contemplative surroundings (tickets: Ⓦ www.lippu.fi or on the door). ⓣ 09 2340 2524 Ⓦ www.kirkkosoikoon.fi

Musica Nova Helsinki Hear important new music at this showcase for Finnish and international contemporary composers. The festival is generally held every other year on odd-numbered years. ⓐ Lasipalatsi, Mannerheimintie 22–24 ⓣ 09 6126 5100 Ⓦ www.musicanova.fi

April

April Jazz/Big Band Jazz Festival Finnish and international performers do their best to avoid the melody in concert halls, restaurants and other relaxed (and even ad hoc) venues. ⓐ Ahertajantie 6 B, Espoo ⓣ 09 455 0003 Ⓦ www.apriljazz.fi

Vappu (30 April) This is Walpurgis Night, cue for one of the biggest parties in Finland, when students gather around Havis Amanda, the mermaid symbol of Helsinki, to drink champagne.

May

Vappupäivä (1 May) The Ullanlinna and Kaisaniemi quarters are the main sites for the lively May Day celebrations, with lots of family-oriented fun, including carnivals.

Evening Markets From mid-May, head to the harbour when dusk falls to discover a host of beautifully presented stalls offering foods, handicrafts and other goods.

June

Helsinki Day (12 June) One of the few European capitals that knows its exact birthday, Helsinki marks the occasion with free concerts at Kaivopuisto Park, plus children's events, sports, tours and a market (see page 47). Ⓦ www.hel.fi

Midsummer Eve Finns celebrate at country homes with huge bonfires, *juhannussalko* poles decorated with ribbons and flowers, and many hours of traditional folk music and dance. For those left in the city, there is a celebration at Seurasaari. Tickets are sold at the Tomtebo Folklore Centre (just before the bridge to Seurasaari) or at the office on the island itself. ❶ 09 4050 9660 Ⓦ www.seurasaarisaatio.fi

July

Jazz Espa Free daily jazz performances on the Esplanadi. ❶ 09 757 2077 Ⓦ www.jazzliitto.fi

Tuska Open Air Metal Festival Major bands from across Europe and the UK play in Kaisaniemi Park. Ⓦ www.tuska-festival.fi

◆ *An audience party at a May Day event*

August

Art Goes Kapakka (mid-August) Ten days of music and entertainment right across the city, totalling 250 performances and events in clubs, bars, restaurants, theatres and streets. Ⓦ www.artgoeskapakka.fi

Helsinki City Marathon Scandinavia's biggest marathon begins at the Paavo Nurmi statue and winds along the shore and hillsides. ⓐ Radiokatu 20 ⓣ 09 3481 2405 Ⓦ www.helsinkicitymarathon.com

Helsinki Festival (late August–early September) Featuring prominent international artists in various venues and a festival tent (tickets: Ⓦ www.lippu.fi). The Night of the Arts brings a wide range of street music and art. ⓣ 09 6126 5100 Ⓦ www.helsinkifestival.fi

Flow Festival A long weekend of music from all over the world combines music genres from jazz to rock and electronic. ⓐ Suvilahti, Kaasutehtaankatu 1 ⓣ 09 670 651 Ⓦ www.flowfestival.com (tickets: ⓣ 0600 1 1616 Ⓦ www.tiketti.fi)

September

Helsinki International Film Festival Finland's largest film festival draws upwards of 14,000 people to see movies of all types from all over the world. ⓐ Mannerheimintie 22-24 ⓣ 09 684 35230 Ⓦ www.hiff.fi

October

Herring Market (early October) Fishermen gather in Kauppatori (Market Square) to sell traditional herring products. A great opportunity to sample local foods and boost your Omega 3 intake.

November

Winter Circus (November–early January) The Hurjaruuth Dance Company at Boiler Hall (Pannuhalli) brings expertise in dance and an

array of performing arts (tickets: Ⓦ www.lippupalvelu.fi). ❸ Cable
Factory, Tallberginkatu 1 ☏ 09 565 7250 Ⓦ www.hurjaruuth.fi

December
Independence Day (6 December) This date kicks off the holiday
season, and is also an occasion for processions, visits to cemeteries
and gatherings in churches and public places for concerts (which
always include Sibelius's *Finlandia*).
St Thomas Christmas Market The finest crafts, foods and arts line
the Esplanadi, set out in colourful tents to engage the interest
of the passer-by (see page 76).
Turku Christmas Market Held in the Old Great Square, with crafts
and foods.
Women's Christmas Fair An astonishing variety of fine crafts,
all created by Finnish women, fill a market hall at the
Wanha Satama (see page 77).

PUBLIC HOLIDAYS
New Year's Day 1 Jan
Epiphany 6 Jan
Easter 22–5 Apr 2011, 6–9 Apr 2012, 29 Mar–1 Apr 2013
May Day 1 May
Ascension Day 2 June 2011, 17 May 2012, 9 May 2013
Midsummer Eve & Midsummer Day 25 & 26 June 2010,
24 & 25 June 2011, 22 & 23 June 2012
All Saints 6 Nov 2010, 5 Nov 2011, 3 Nov 2012
Independence Day 6 Dec
Christmas 24–6 Dec

The National Romantics

Finland's version of Romantic Nationalism was similar to other countries' in that it sprang from a desire for independence. By the turn of the 20th century, the people we know as the Finns were reacting against years of control, first by the Swedes, and then by Russia. Their wish for an identity and cultural heritage of their own focused primarily on the *Kalevala*, a national saga that was a compendium of folk tales from the rural heartland of Karelia. These stories' motifs and themes, which are evident in Finnish culture today, were met by an influx of new ideas that came from the European Arts and Crafts Movement and the art nouveau aesthetic; this synthesis of ancient and modern cultural phenomena resulted in the emergence of a group of brilliant young artists. Among them were Jean Sibelius (whose *Finlandia* is a pure expression of national pride) and the painters Akseli Gallen-Kallela and Helene Schjerfbeck.

Pre-eminent among them, though, were the architects Herman Gesellius, Armas Lindgren and Eliel Saarinen, who met at Helsinki's Polytechnic Institute, formed a consultancy, and soon began to wield an immense influence on the local, national and international stages. The trio developed Jugendstil (Finnish for 'art nouveau') architecture into a style called National Romantic, a form that was directly influenced by the Karelian architectural heritage. They designed some of Helsinki's most prominent buildings, such as the Ateneum and Helsinki Railway Station (see pages 71 & 66). Finnish National Romanticism really came to the world's attention at the Paris World Exposition of 1900 (at which time Finland was still a Grand Duchy of the Russian Empire), thanks to the sensation caused by the drama, dynamism and dash of Saarinen's Pavilion. In fact, Paris 1900 almost certainly marks the birth of what the world would come to admire as Finnish design, which, despite the fact that the Finns' independence has removed the catalyst of artistic urgency, has prospered and evolved, and, some might allege, reached its zenith thus far with the Nokia N97 phone. Or was it the Oma lemon squeezer?

🔺 *Elegant 19th-century Finnish architecture on the Esplanadi*

History

At a latitude of 60° north, Helsinki is the northernmost of all
continental European capitals, with a prime location on the Baltic.
Its historical position as the bridge between Russia and the West
made Finland a pawn between the rulers of Sweden – Scandinavia's
most aggressive power – and Russia. During Swedish rule the
provincial capital was at Turku; it was Swedish King Gustav Vasa
who established a trading port at Helsinki in 1550.

This busy port settlement gradually grew in importance, until
the early 1700s dealt it a double blow: in 1710 the plague nearly
wiped out its 2,000 inhabitants; then, in 1713, the Swedes burned
it down to keep it from falling into the hands of Peter the Great.
To protect the harbour from future attacks, Sweden built the great
Suomenlinna Fortress (see page 110). However, Russian harassment
continued to slow the city's growth.

A century after the plague, two more events changed Helsinki
irrevocably. A fire in 1808 devastated most of the city and, before
it was rebuilt, the province was ceded to Russia in 1809, ending
Swedish rule. Finland became the semi-autonomous Russian Grand
Duchy of Finland, and Tsar Alexander I lavished attention on his new
city on the Baltic. He brought in the German-born architect C L Engel,
who had designed much of St Petersburg. Engel remodelled Helsinki,
especially around Senate Square, and gave it the elegance that it
retains today. In 1812 Alexander I moved the capital of the Grand
Duchy from Turku to Helsinki, and the city has been the capital
ever since.

Rapid industrialisation from the 1860s to the beginning of the
20th century meant equally rapid population growth, and with it
came the need for new neighbourhoods. Building after building

sprang out of this boom, especially at the turn of the century, when Helsinki acquired a remarkable number of art nouveau structures by such luminaries as Eliel Saarinen, Armas Lindgren and their contemporaries. At the same time, a feeling of growing nationalism pushed the country toward independence.

Finland seized the moment when revolution rocked Russia in 1917: Parliament declared independence on 6 December and, after a short civil war, a republic was declared in 1919, with Helsinki as its capital. Since then, with the exception of the period of war with the Soviet Union in the 1940s, Helsinki has grown as an industrial and innovatory centre at the forefront of the Scandinavian design phenomenon. Since the 1952 Olympics it has also been a centre for major sporting events, and a prime location for the development of international diplomatic initiatives. Since 1995 Finland has been a member of the European Union. The country's first female president, Tarja Halonen, has been in power since 2001. The next presidential election will be held in 2012.

🔺 *The ordeal of World War II is commemorated at Hietaniemi Cemetery*

Lifestyle

It was the Finns who invented the sauna, despite what jealousy may lead other Scandinavians to allege. For most Finns, the chance to relax in extreme heat is one of life's civilising rituals, and they're likely to fit one in at any time of day, as the urge takes them. Saunas are the venues for business meetings, family gatherings and all kinds of social interplay, which explains why they're found all over the

⬤ *Out and about in the occasional snowstorm*

city, sometimes in the unlikeliest of locations. Proximity to a lake is a definite bonus, since the Finns are great believers in a quick plunge into cold water after – or during – a sauna.

Though often believed to be taciturn, the Finns can actually be quite voluble in social situations, especially when loosened up with a little alcohol. They also have a wicked sense of humour, which is often very dry and sly, along with a keen sense of the ridiculous. They can laugh at themselves, and their apparent self-deprecation is a popular national joke with them. It is true, however, that a group of Finns can sit in a room together quite happily without uttering a word, and be quite comfortable. So don't be alarmed if silence appears to descend the very minute you enter almost any social setting. And expect silence in the sauna, unless you're in a business meeting. By the way, saunas are always gender-divided, except for those owned or popularly used by families. The same is true of the nude beaches in Helsinki, which you will find at Seurasaari and on Pihlajasaari. Women and men each have separate sections of beach on which to frolic, giggle and go all shrivelled.

Finns are generally easy-going and have a live-and-let-live attitude, so although Helsinki doesn't have the gay scene of, say, Stockholm, gay travellers are welcome and excite little attention. There are several gay clubs in the city, but at most of them heterosexual couples are welcome. When it comes to clothes, Finns are usually casual, though they like to put their glad rags on for a big night out. They dress for the climate, so it's not unusual to see boots and thick ski jackets in the cloakrooms of upmarket restaurants in the winter. The Finns are pretty sensible people, who don't get huffy over dress codes or have bouncers to protect self-consciously cool venues from the criminally under-preened. The Finns go out to have a good time, and they are happy for you to have a good time, too.

Culture

The fact that Finland has such a distinct culture of its own is remarkable, considering that this small country spent so much of its past being tossed back and forth between two other – and very strong – cultures. That the Finnish language has remained distinct and in steady use is equally surprising. Today, just enough of the Russian and Swedish flavours remain in Finnish culture to make things interesting.

What does predominate is the Finnish sense of style. Leaders in modern design, the Finns are the epitome of the Scandinavian aesthetic – clean lines, fresh concepts and functional designs that look sharp and work well. Whether it's a building, a mobile phone, sportswear or a kitchen appliance, if it's designed in Finland, it will combine the often-conflicting needs of form and function into one graceful whole. Interest in design is more than a trade commodity, it's a national passion, because the Finns genuinely revel in being surrounded by well-designed things, whether they are the world's most comfortable scissors (Fiskars) or stylish home accessories (Marimekko or Arabia).

Helsinki's Design District (see page 62) is the place to revel in this Finnish phenomenon. In the space of a few streets, you'll find the Design Museum (see page 72), the Museum of Finnish Architecture (see page 75) and the Design Forum (see page 77), as well as galleries and designer shops.

Other arts hold a high place in Finnish culture, too. Foreigners may be surprised to see enthusiastic fans of all ages in audiences at the opera or symphony. Finns are likely to have the works of Finnish artists hanging on their walls. Finland's architects are world famous, and the Finns value their creativity just as much as the rest of the

◆ *Marimekko is one of the most famous Finnish design brands*

A RACE APART

Although Finland is most definitely a Scandinavian country, and culturally has gained a lot from its long connection with Sweden, the Finns are not primarily of the same northern Germanic stock as their Scandinavian neighbours, and their language is also distinct. No-one knows for sure how long the Finns have been living in the Baltic or exactly where their ancestors came from, but the Finnish language belongs to a group that includes Estonian and Hungarian, and is entirely unrelated to the Indo-European languages that nearly all of the rest of Europe speaks.

world, so you'll see examples of their work at every turn. Helsinki residents are far more likely to know the name of a local building's architect than residents of any other city in Europe.

Helsinki is filled with performance venues for everything from opera and dance to rock concerts and sports competitions. Tickets are refreshingly well priced – those for the Philharmonic Orchestra concerts cost between €5 and €15, for example. For tickets to various concert and theatre venues, contact **Lippupalvelu** (❶ 0600 1 08 00 or 0600 10 020 Ⓦ www.lippupalvelu.fi), or **Tiketti** (❶ 0600 1 16 16 Ⓦ www.tiketti.fi). For other listings media, see page 32.

❍ *Tourists admiring the Helsinki view from the steps of the Lutheran Cathedral*

MAKING THE MOST OF
Helsinki

Shopping

The streets bordering the Esplanadi and the parallel Aleksanterinkatu lead to Mannerheimintie, forming the centre of Helsinki's most fashionable (and pricey) shopping district. Just beyond lies the Design District (see page 62) where you'll find designer shops selling everything from paper clips to coffee pots, and Fredrikinkatu, lined with boutiques and music shops. In the morning market at the harbour (see page 68), you'll find fresh local farm products, crafts and Russian fur hats, with more foods sold in the striped market hall. Another market is at Hakaniemi (see page 79), which has crafts on the upper floor. At the western edge of the city is the restored Hietalahti market hall and a giant flea market (see page 97), where you can get anything from last year's clothing to family heirlooms – all at cheap prices.

Shops are generally open from 09.00 or 10.00 to 18.00 or 20.00 Monday to Friday and 09.00 to 14.00 Saturday. Most close Sundays, though major department stores often open on Sundays from June to August and before Christmas.

Distinctive Finnish products to look for are glassware (big names are Iittala, Nuutajärvi and Arabia), clothing of fur and leather, traditional and contemporary jumpers and jerseys, and beautiful wooden utensils and furnishings. Exquisite kitchenware, carved in graceful and flowing forms of velvet-smooth local woods, includes spoons, spatulas and cake servers. Foods you may want to take back with you after you've tasted them are cloudberry or lingonberry preserves, smoked reindeer or salmon, and the incomparable Finnish honey.

Local crafts, found in handwork and museum shops and in markets, vary widely. Rustic reindeer made of bundled straw or hand-knitted traditional woollen hats, socks and mittens are sold alongside the sleek, modern designs for which Scandinavia is so well known. In Helsinki's shops you'll find Sámi crafts from Lapland, such as reindeer-bone jewellery and carved birchwood cups. Look for the *duodji* label, guaranteeing that these are genuine Sámi crafts.

The good news for non-European shoppers is that Finland's 22 per cent VAT is often refundable for those who are not residents of the European Union. The easiest way to avoid receiving separate euro cheques from each shop (these may cost you more than their value to cash) is to use Global Refund Service. Ask for a refund cheque at any shop displaying a 'Tax Free' logo. At the airport, have these stamped at the Global Refund Desk and collect your refund in cash.

USEFUL SHOPPING PHRASES

What time do they open/close?
Milloin se avataan/suljetan?
Mil-loin she ervertahn/suljehtahn?

How much is it?
Paljonko se maksaa?
Perlyonko she merksah?

I'd like to buy ...
Haluaisin ostaa ...
Herlu-aisin ostah ...

Eating & drinking

It's true that Finnish cuisine has not yet rocked the European charts, but several of Helsinki's chefs certainly have. The best of them revel in the ingredients of the surrounding water and land – seafood from the Baltic and from Finland's lakes, vegetables and berries whose flavours have concentrated as they ripen in the long hours of summer sun, wild berries from the north, mushrooms gathered from the forests, and game from the tundra and fells. A number of Helsinki's restaurants offer special seasonal menus of these local ingredients at the height of their season, as part of an initiative called HelsinkiMenu.

Complicated preparations are shunned in favour of those that let the natural flavours of fresh ingredients shine through. Chefs draw on the traditional influences of Finland, Russia and Sweden, as well as an eclectic mix that ranges from Asian to Mediterranean. While you can find French, Italian, Chinese, Thai and even Irish pub food here, you'll eat best when you seek Finnish chefs working with their own native ingredients.

Meals are normally served in three courses, often beginning with a warming hearty soup in the winter. Pork, lamb and beef are common main-course meats, and many menus offer reindeer in some form. Bear is usually served in Russian restaurants (Helsinki's are known

PRICE CATEGORIES
Price ratings for restaurants in this book are based on the average cost of a main course for one person.
£ up to €15   ££ €15–25   £££ over €25

◯ *Finns make the most of the summer by eating outdoors as much as possible*

for being better than those in St Petersburg), as a stew or smoked.

Baltic herring, *silakka*, is the favourite fish, fried, grilled, baked with layers of potato and cream or pickled as a snack. Herring is also smoked or marinated in a way similar to *gravadlax*, which is made with salmon. Arctic char, trout, salmon and whitefish are popular, and crayfish are in season during August and September.

In the autumn, markets are piled high with woodland mushrooms (mostly) from Lapland, and chefs take full advantage of this bounteous supply. Chanterelles are the tastiest of these, but you'll see all sorts, in meat dishes or served on their own.

Sausages (*makkara*) are the snack food of choice, and you'll find them sizzling on grills in markets and street stalls. They may be made from pork or any other meat, and are always delicious. *Mustamakkara* is a black sausage from Tampere, and is usually served with sweet-tart lingonberry jam.

Lingonberries and the earthy-sweet cloudberries ripen in the autumn, but you'll find them as jams and condiments and in desserts any time of year. Cloudberries are an especially rare delicacy, but they will be on the menus of better restaurants, frequently as a topping for puddings and ice cream. Pastries and baked goods are excellent, and the Finns enjoy these with their coffee at cafés and bakeries. Sweet coffee breads are popular, as is *karjalanpiirakat*, a savoury pastry from eastern Finland, with a filling of rice. Breads are varied and very good, ranging from dark rye to a snowy-white bread made with potatoes. Crisp flatbreads are usually made of rye flour.

Breads are always part of a full breakfast (a meal that is usually quite hearty), with a hot dish of eggs and meat and often porridge, or a buffet of cold cuts and cheeses – and plenty of coffee, although tea will always be available.

Wine is available at most restaurants, with some, such as Ravintola Carelia & Winebar (see page 103) and G W Sundmans (see page 84), having outstanding wine lists. Local alcoholic drinks include vodka, schnapps and liqueurs made from local berries. Look especially for *lakka*, made of cloudberries, and *mesimarja*, made of highly flavoured Arctic brambleberries. Or try Salmari, a potent and extremely popular pre-mixed vodka cocktail. If you prefer beer, a good local one to try is Lapin Kulta. In the winter you'll be offered *glögi*, a tasty blend of red wine, spices, raisins, almonds and blackcurrant juice. There are as many recipes for this as there are people making it, some using white wine. At any winter market, you'll find at least one steaming black cauldron of *glögi*.

Breakfast is normally served from 07.00 to 10.00, and lunch begins early, at 11.00. The evening meal is also served early, often from 16.00 or 17.00, but continues late into the evening, with many restaurants serving until 23.00. The midday meal may be a light lunch or a full meal. The latter is often a bargain, at a set price as low as €8. Advance booking is wise for popular restaurants, especially on Wednesday, Friday and Saturday evenings. If meeting Finnish friends for a meal (or any other occasion), remember that they are prompt and value punctuality. If you are delayed for more than five minutes, phone them – they will be carrying a mobile.

Service charges are usually included in restaurant bills, but a modest tip is always welcome if service has been attentive. Give this directly to the server in cash, rather than adding it to the bill. Smoking is banned in public places.

USEFUL DINING PHRASES

I would like a table for ... people
Saadaanko me pöytä ...
Sahdahnko meh per-ewta ...

May I see the menu?
Voisinko nähdä menun?
Voi-shinko nahkh-da mehnun?

I am a vegetarian
Olen kasvissyöjä
Olehn kers-vis-sewer-ya

May I have the bill?
Saisinko laskun?
Sai-sinko lerksun?

Where is the toilet (restroom)?
Missa on vessa?
Missa on vessah?

Entertainment & nightlife

With almost 10 per cent of its population being university students, Helsinki is among Europe's hippest cities, with non-stop nightlife that's all the better for being largely undiscovered by foreigners. Don't worry about feeling left out, though, since almost everyone under 40 speaks excellent English. Variety is the name of Helsinki's game, with everything from clubs run by film directors to jazz clubs, gay clubs, raucous pubs and heavy-metal karaoke bars.

Without, perhaps, the pretension of Stockholm, but with all its variety and cool, Helsinki's night scene is user-friendly. There are no dress codes here – you'll want to be smartly dressed, but no ties are required and, as we've said, no bouncers will be at the door selecting clientele on the basis of their designer labels. Age is another matter, since clubs set their own rules. If you're over 24, you're home free; between 20 and 24 you may not be allowed into some clubs, especially on busy nights. A few places welcome anyone over 18, especially in the area around the Kamppi metro station, a popular area for under-20s.

The hot nights are Friday and Saturday, but Wednesday is also often busy. Expect to pay about €5 for admission to clubs, more for those with live music, plus another €1–2 for the compulsory coat check. A glass of beer or wine is usually about €4–5.

Nightlife is hottest in the streets around the railway station (unlike in many other cities, this area is prime real estate), along the Esplanadi and immediately south, between Mannerheimintie and Fredrikinkatu, west of Mannerheimintie between Finlandia Hall and the opera, and in the streets south of Uudenmaankatu, as far as Kapteeninkatu. An up-and-coming area for pubs is Kallio, where the previously grungy atmosphere is becoming increasingly hip.

Do be aware that Finns can become belligerent when drunk,

and fights may break out as night fades into morning. So if the atmosphere begins to take on an angry tone, slip quietly away, and under no circumstances engage a drunk in an argument or take chances with a potentially insulting remark. And if someone insults you, ignore them and leave as soon as possible.

Clubs are not the only place young Finns spend a night out. Live performances are everywhere: arena rock shows, experimental metal, pop and a summer packed with festivals that always include music, often free. Besides the highbrow halls for opera, ballet and classical music (all well attended by people of all ages), venues include the **Savoy Theatre** (ⓐ Kasarminkatu 46 ⓣ 09 3101 2000 ⓦ www.savoyteatteri.fi) for stage performances by Finnish and touring companies that range from classical theatre to contemporary and occasional musical shows; Olympic Stadium (see page 88), home to all the big summer concerts; and the somewhat smaller **Hartwall Areena** (ⓐ Areenakuja ⓣ 0204 1997 ⓦ www.hartwall-areena.com), where even headliners like Metallica, Depeche Mode and Elton John perform. At the smaller **House of Culture** (ⓐ Sturenkatu 4 ⓣ 09 774 0270 ⓦ www.kulttuuritalo.fi) you'll hear metal, rock and pop.

Another good option for a relatively cheap and cheerful night out, particularly if it's raining or you're with children, is the cinema. Cinema programmes are available from hotels and the tourist office. The widest choice is at Tennispalatsi (see page 105) with 14 screens, and **Kinopalatsi** (ⓐ Kaisaniemenkatu 2 ⓣ 0600 007 007 ⓦ www.finnkino.fi), with ten. The selection is international and all films are shown in their original language with Finnish subtitles. Soundtracks are very rarely dubbed. **The Orion** (ⓐ Eerikinkatu 15 ⓣ 09 615 400 ⓦ www.kava.fi) is home to the Finnish Film Archive, which shows three films every day except

Mondays. Tickets at the major cinemas are about €10 for evening shows; smaller venues cost less. Book ahead for Friday and Saturday evenings.

Before you travel to Helsinki, it's worth finding out what's on during your stay and booking tickets if necessary. Helsinki City Tourist & Convention Bureau (see page 153) has up-to-date information on what's happening at all venues, including clubs. Before you go, visit Ⓦ www.visithelsinki.fi, and click on 'brochures' to download publications filled with the latest news on what's hot in entertainment and clubs. *Nordic Oddity* contains insider tips.

When you arrive in Helsinki, pick up a copy of the twice-monthly *City Lehti* for listings of current happenings – it's free at most shops and hotels. *Helsinki This Week*, the tourist office's magazine in English, is also free, and available everywhere. It is stronger on restaurant information and has a good calendar of events for the current month, in addition to seasonal features. For a complete listing of the many summer music festivals in Finland, see Ⓦ www.festivals.fi.

Tickets for events at most major venues are available through either Lippupalvelu or Tiketti (see page 22).

● *Helsinki has a wealth of exciting live performance venues*

Sport & relaxation

Don't abandon your fitness routines in Helsinki – this is an exercise-friendly, go-for-it town, with parks and paths everywhere. The Finns are great walkers, runners, skiers, skaters and cyclists, so this is a good way to mingle with locals, too.

PARTICIPATION SPORTS

Jogging & cycling The most popular jogging routes are around Töölö Bay and the shore at Vanhankaupunginkoski (Old Town Rapids). To enjoy the network of bike paths between sights, borrow a free City Bike (€2 deposit) from any of the green racks.

Winter sports In winter, you can also rent ski equipment and snowshoes at the Töölö centre and go on your own or take a guided hike – call ❶ 09 228 81500 or see ⓦ www.helsinkiexpert.fi for details. The **Paloheinä Recreational Centre** (ⓐ Pakilantie 124 ❶ 09 8775 2281 ⓦ Bus: 66, 66A) also offers rental skis, boots and poles. Trails, lit after

◔ All of Helsinki's large parks have ski trails

dark, open as early as November and may have snow into April. Skating rinks are everywhere, but the **Kallion Tekojäärata** (ⓐ Helsinginkatu 23 ⓣ 09 3103 1643 ⓛ Mid-Nov–mid-Mar ⓝ Tram: 1A, 3B, 8) and the **Helsinki Icepark** (ⓐ Next to train station on Rautatientori ⓣ 040 334 5617 ⓦ www.jaapuisto.fi ⓛ Late Nov–mid Mar) have music and rental skates.

Fishing All that sparkling clean water surrounding the city will tempt anglers, and all they need is a traveller's fishing permit from Stockmann department store (see page 79) or a fishing shop. The shore around the Old Town Rapids is reserved for fishing. See ⓦ www.ahven.net for further information.

RELAXATION

Swimming & saunas The Olympic-size pools at the **Swimming Stadium** (ⓐ Hammerskjöldintie 5 ⓣ 09 3108 7854 ⓛ May–mid-Sept ⓝ Tram: 3T, 7) and the **Mäkelänrinne Swimming Centre** (ⓐ Makelankatu 49 ⓣ 09 3484 8800 ⓦ www.urheiluhallit.fi ⓛ 06.15–21.00 Mon–Fri, 08.00–20.00 Sat, 09.00–20.00 Sun ⓝ Tram: 1, 1A, 7) are open to the public, or you can combine swimming with a real cultural fix at Helsinki's oldest traditional swimming hall, the **Yrjönkatu Swimming Hall** (ⓐ Yrjonkatu 21 ⓣ 09 3108 7401), which also has a sauna. Bathing suits are not worn here, so men and women swim at different times; the schedule is available at most hotels. The best beaches are at Seurasaari, Suomenlinna and Pihlajasaari.

Of course, you shouldn't miss the most Finnish of all activities – a sauna. The 70-year-old **Kotiharjun** (ⓐ Harjutorinkatu 1 ⓣ 09 753 1535 ⓦ www.kotiharjunsauna.fi) is Helsinki's last old-fashioned wood-burning (as opposed to electric) sauna, which makes for an interesting twist. For more options in Helsinki, visit ⓦ www.sauna.fi. Or for the ultimate luxury, steal away to the Naantali Spa, near Turku (see page 140).

Accommodation

For a Scandinavian capital, Helsinki offers some surprisingly moderate hotel rates. Of course, you can luxuriate in grandeur, but there are more budget options here than in many other Nordic cities. Even the finest hotels, such as the Hotel Kämp, offer special promotions, especially at weekends. Always ask about these when booking.

Most hotels are centrally located, and nearly all are close to public transportation. Unlike in many other cities, you needn't worry about staying close to the railway station, since this is an excellent neighbourhood in the midst of the best shopping and attractions.

A **Helsinki Expert** (☎ 09 2288 1400 ⓦ www.helsinkiexpert.fi 🕐 09.00–18.00 Mon–Fri, 10.00–18.00 Sat & Sun, June–Aug; 09.00–18.00 Mon–Fri, 10.00–17.00 Sat, Sept–May) booking service is located at the railway station and handles hotels, hostels and smaller guest houses. For information on hostels, contact the **Finnish Youth Hostel Association** (ⓦ www.srm.fi).

HOTELS

Finn £ Just over half a kilometre (a third of a mile) from the railway station, this is a small but comfortable hotel and reasonably priced. All 27 rooms have private facilities, TV and phone, and some have a shower. A pool and saunas are next door. ❸ Kalevankatu 3 B (Western & northern Helsinki) ☎ 09 684 4360 ⓦ www.hotellifinn.fi Ⓜ Metro: Kamppi

Arthur £–££ A handsome and recently refurbished small hotel within a few hundred metres of the railway station and the best shopping. Weekend rates for a standard double are under €100. The on-site

PRICE CATEGORIES
Price ratings for accommodation are based on the average rate
for a double room for one night (usually including breakfast).
£ up to €80   ££ €80–175   £££ over €175

restaurant is well regarded. ➋ Vuorikatu 19 (Esplanadi & the Harbour)
➊ 09 173 441 ⓦ www.hotelarthur.fi Ⓜ Metro: Kaisaniemi

Crowne Plaza Helsinki ££ The Crowne Plaza is a large, multi-storey,
modern, glass-fronted building at the very heart of city life. The
beautifully appointed modern rooms have everything, including
high-speed internet connections. The fitness facilities, including
a large pool, are impressive, too. ➋ Mannerheimintie 50 (Western &
northern Helsinki) ➊ 09 252 10000 ⓦ www.crowneplaza-helsinki.fi
Ⓜ Metro: Rautatientori; tram: 4, 7, 10

Cumulus Kaisaniemi ££ Another business travel hotel, close to
downtown. Clean, comfortable and friendly. ➋ Kaisaniemenkatu 7
(Esplanadi & the Harbour) ➊ 09 172 881 ⓦ www.cumulus.fi
Ⓜ Metro: Kaisaniemi

Cumulus Olympia ££ A sister hotel to the Kaisaniemi, this is a
good choice if you're interested in athletics. It's near the Olympic
Stadium, and bowling, swimming and ball games are available at
the Urheilutalo Sports Centre next door. It's also close to Linnanmäki
Amusement Park and Sea Life Helsinki. ➋ Läntinen Brahenkatu 2
(Islands & outskirts) ➊ 09 691 51 ⓦ www.cumulus.fi Ⓜ Tram: 1A, 3B, 8

Haaga ££ Large and modern, this hotel is about 5 km (3 miles) from the centre but is served by a frequent bus service. Golfers note: Tali golf course is only 4 km (2½ miles) away. ⓐ Nuijamiestentie 10 (Islands & outskirts) ⓣ 09 580 7877 ⓦ www.bestwestern.com ⓝ Bus: 63

Helka ££ Rooms at this centrally located hotel were recently refurbished with funky décor and furniture; all have private bathrooms, TV and phones. Further facilities include saunas and a whirlpool for relaxation, and a bar and restaurant. It's a business hotel, so rates are reduced at weekends. ⓐ Pohjoinen Rautatiekatu 23 (Western & northern Helsinki) ⓣ 09 613 580 ⓦ www.helka.fi ⓝ Metro: Kamppi

Hotel Katajanokka ££–£££ A truly unique chance to spend a night in jail without breaking the law. This former prison was turned into a luxury hotel in 2007. ⓐ Vyökatu 1 (Esplanadi & the Harbour) ⓣ 09 686 450 ⓦ www.bwkatajanokka.fi ⓝ Tram: 4T

Linna ££–£££ An elegant boutique hotel in an old art nouveau mansion right in the centre of Helsinki. It has three saunas within its thick granite walls as well as a pétanque court. ⓐ Lönnrotinkatu 29 (Western & northern Helsinki) ⓣ 010 3444 100 ⓦ www.palacekamp.fi ⓝ Tram: 6

Scandic Grand Marina ££–£££ This hotel, in a brilliantly converted 1913 warehouse designed by architect Lars Sonck, boasts elegant modern rooms. Excellent location on the harbour, opposite the ferry terminal. ⓐ Katajanokanlaituri 7 (Esplanadi & the Harbour) ⓣ 09 16 661 ⓦ www.scandichotels.fi ⓝ Tram: 4

● *Hotel Glo is one of the city's best hotels*

Glo £££ This new boutique hotel offers 144 sleekly designed, generously sized rooms with trendy extras such as flat-screen TVs and Wi-Fi. Staff go out of their way to accommodate special requests. Carlito's gourmet pizzeria serves carefully designed pizzas with first class ingredients. ⓐ Kluuvikatu 4 (Esplanadi & the Harbour) ⓣ 010 3444 400 ⓦ www.palacekamp.fi ⓜ Metro: Kaisaniemi

Hotel Kämp £££ Stunningly restored, this grand hotel dating from 1887 has service to match, with facilities such as a day spa. The location, near the Esplanadi, is superb, and the breakfast buffet outstanding. ⓐ Pohjoisesplanadi 29 (Esplanadi & the Harbour) ⓣ 09 5840 9520 ⓦ www.hotelkamp.fi ⓜ Tram: 3T, 4, 7

Rivoli Jardin £££ Close to the Esplanadi and to the activities of the central district, this elegant, family-run boutique hotel has 55 rooms, plus a wide range of business features including internet access. There's also an on-site sauna. Apartments are available and you can even bring your dog. ⓐ Kasarmikatu 40 (Esplanadi & the Harbour) ⓣ 09 681 500 ⓦ www.rivoli.fi ⓜ Tram: 9, 10

HOSTELS
Eurohostel £ This hostel has 255 beds in 135 rooms; singles, doubles, triples and family rooms are available. The recently repainted rooms have TVs and new furniture, and there are self-catering facilities on each floor. Rates include a morning sauna. Shared bathrooms. ⓐ Linnankatu 9 (Western & northern Helsinki) ⓣ 09 6220470 ⓦ www.eurohostel.fi ⓜ Tram: 4

Hostel Suomenlinna £ If the idea of staying in a fortress appeals, this is the place for you. A fascinating sight in itself, the island fortress (see page 110) was built by the Swedes and reinforced by the Russians as a primary defence for the city. The hostel has 40 beds, in rooms for between two and ten people, plus a café and self-catering kitchen. Showers and toilets are shared. It's only a 15-minute ferry ride from the city centre. ⓐ Suomenlinna C 9 (The islands & outskirts) ① 09 684 7471 Ⓦ www.leirikoulut.com Ⓝ Ferry from Kauppatori

Stadion Hostel £ A friendly, comfortable hostel in the Olympic Stadium. There are 167 beds, available in dormitories or in private rooms. There's a shared kitchen but breakfast is also offered. ⓐ Pohjoinen Stadiontie 4 ① 09 477 8480 (Western & northern Helsinki) Ⓦ www.stadionhostel.com Ⓝ Tram: 3T, 4, 7A (get off at Aurora Hospital)

CAMPSITE
Rastila Camping Camping in the city is possible here, a 15–20 minute ride from the railway station. The on-site restaurant is open in summer. ⓐ Karavaanikatu 4 ① 09 310 78517 Ⓦ www.rastilacamping.fi Ⓝ Metro: Rastila

THE BEST OF HELSINKI

If you only have a few days to spend in Helsinki, you may be tempted to concentrate on the eastern half of the city centre, but you should try to make time to take in some of the sights of the western and northern areas and definitely take a harbour trip to see this fascinating metropolis from a different angle.

TOP 10 ATTRACTIONS

- **Suomenlinna Fortress** One of the world's largest sea fortresses and a World Heritage Site to boot on an island out in the harbour (see page 110)

- **Boat trips around the archipelago** Admire the city from all angles on an excursion boat or a ferry trip to the islands (see page 106)

- **Uspenski Cathedral** The Russian presence of western Europe's largest Orthodox church still makes an impression (see page 70)

- **Kauppatori (Market Square) and Harbour** The real heart of Helsinki, where locals, visitors, craftspeople and traders meet (see page 68)

- **Design Museum** The evolution of style periods expressed in numerous materials and objects. Brilliant design, brilliantly displayed (see page 72)

- **Art nouveau buildings** Take a walking tour around Helsinki's fabulous art nouveau architecture (see page 64)

- **Seurasaari Open-air Museum** Historic buildings from all over Finland are here at this island museum with its working farm (see page 114)

- **Korkeasaari Zoo** Snow leopards, Amur and Siberian tigers, Asian lions: big cat heaven (see page 109)

- **Temppeliaukio Church** The church in a rock – come here for wonderful concerts (see page 91)

- **Finnish design** The latest and coolest – see it first in the Design District around Diana Park (see page 62)

The Pohjola Building, design by Eliel Saarinen, sculptures by Hilda Flodin

Suggested itineraries

HALF-DAY: HELSINKI IN A HURRY

If you're unlucky enough to have only half a day free, you can still use it to absorb a lot of the sights and sounds of the city. Begin at the market, right on the harbour, for a preview of what you'll see on tonight's menu and to mix with the hearty, good-humoured Finns. Make a detour east to see the interior of Uspenski Cathedral (see page 70) before heading uphill from the market to Senaatintori (Senate Square, see page 70). Head west on Aleksanterinkatu, past the smart shops, stepping into no. 44, the Pohjola Insurance Building (see page 68), for a dose of Finnish art nouveau. Don't miss the big square bordered by the National Theatre (see page 75), the Ateneum (see page 71) and Saarinen's landmark railway station (see page 66). Beyond the station, take a left on Mannerheimintie, then left again to circle back to the harbour along the Esplanadi (see page 64). This walk will take you to some more landmark sights, the best of Helsinki's shops and some great cafes (Engel on Senate Square or Café Kappeli on the Esplanadi (see page 81) are local favourites).

1 DAY: TIME TO SEE A LITTLE MORE

If you have completed the morning's whistle-stop tour and have acquired a feel for the architecture, design and lively buzz of the city, use the afternoon to take a boat to the fortress island of Suomenlinna (see page 110). The 15-minute trip gives good city views, and once you're on the island you can explore the fortress buildings, watch the excellent film, visit the museums and craft studios, and walk the island paths for views of the city, surrounding islands, and the ships in the Gulf of Finland. In the evening, treat yourself to a dinner in one of Helsinki's restaurants specialising in local ingredients. Then hit the streets around Fredrikinkatu to learn what real nightlife is.

2–3 DAYS: TIME TO SEE MUCH MORE

You can add a lot more experiences if you have another day or two. The first stop should be the Design Museum (see page 72), after which you will want to wander in the city's exciting Design District to see what's at the cutting edge before it hits the shops all over Europe. Don't miss the Design Forum (see page 77), where you can find top designers' work in all price ranges. Window-shop your way north on Fredrikinkatu or take a bus to Temppeliaukio Church, carved out of solid rock. Head back east toward the unmissable tower of the National Museum (see page 74) and Finlandia Hall (see page 73), opposite, before returning to the centre along busy Mannerheimintie. If you have another day, spend it visiting some of the excellent museums or head for the islands: either the open-air museum of Seurasaari (see pages 114) or the Korkeasaari Zoo (see page 109) to see rare big cats, including snow leopards and Siberian tigers.

LONGER: ENJOYING HELSINKI TO THE FULL

A longer stay gives enough time to head out of the city for a day in old Porvoo or one of the many cruises among the islands. Or combine the two by cruising to Porvoo. After pounding the pavements for a few days, you'll be ready to relax in one of Helsinki's parks, where you can snowshoe or ski in the winter and walk or cycle in the summer. After that, you'll be ready for the other Finnish obsession, a sauna. If your hotel doesn't offer one, choose one of the city's public saunas and join the Finns as they relax.

Something for nothing

Attending one of Helsinki's free festivals doesn't just save on money, but it's also a great way to mingle with locals, enjoy music and be part of Finnish life. However, since the majority take place during the most popular tourist season, you need to book accommodation early.

The ultimate in syncretism is the confluence of Walpurgis Night (itself coinciding with pagan rites of spring), May Day, International Workers' Day and Finland's Student Day (celebrating graduation).

● *Students crowd into Senate Square to celebrate Student Day*

The city welcomes spring (even if the day brings a late snowstorm) in a most un-Finnish way, by becoming one giant block party, with champagne, picnics and bands of liberated students wearing white hats. A cap is placed ceremoniously on the statue of Havis Amanda on the evening of 30 April, and champagne flows – along with the goodwill – well into the night and all the next day.

The last weekend in May brings the **World Village Festival** (ⓦ www.maailmakylassa.fi), two days of free stage performances, exhibitions, street musicians and sports in Kaisaniemi Park. Several stages feature performers from all over the world, many of them emerging artists that go on to become famous. Past performances have included Sengalese hip-hop, Chilean reggae, Finnish folk rock and a Spanish ska/rock/flamenco/Rai group. Exotic food, folk crafts and exhibition booths add to the atmosphere, with an international buzz filling the city.

Helsinki-päivä, Helsinki Day, celebrates the city's birthday on 12 June, with free concerts, a three-day samba and dance festival with cruises, tours and free entrance to museums. It ends with a rock concert in Kaivopuisto Park, (close to the British and United States Embassies, off Puistokatu). There are market stalls on the Esplanadi, free performances on the Espa stage all day and free admission to Suomenlinna Fortress. It is especially good for families with children, as it is relatively alcohol-free.

Most summer weekends bring Alppipuisto (next to the Linnanmäki Amusement Park) alive with music, free of charge. For a week in mid-August, the Art Goes Kapakka festival also offers a wide range of free entertainment in the bars of Helsinki. Night of the Arts takes place on a Friday in late August, with museums and galleries staying open until late at night and the streets coming alive with free musical performances.

When it rains

Helsinki is such an outdoor city, filled with leafy parks, broad
avenues, street markets and pedestrianised shopping streets,
that most travellers spend much of their time outside enjoying the
long daylight hours. Three of its most famous sights – Suomenlinna
Fortress, Seurasaari and Korkeasaari Zoo – are open-air attractions.
But a whole layer of the city is so hidden that even multi-time visitors
might not know it exists under their feet. Beneath the streets of
the city centre, from the railway station to the Esplanadi, under
Mannerheimintie to the Forum, and as far west as the Kamppi
bus station, lies a maze of connected underground passages lined
with shops, cafés, restaurants, bakeries and food markets. Street
musicians play, and escalators and stairs connect to the department
stores, shopping centres and services above.

The tunnels even offer direct access to transportation, connecting
the train and bus stations and city transit lines. In cold or rainy weather
you can spend a whole day shopping or browsing in the subterranean
shops, the department stores of Stockmann and Sokos, the trendy
shops of the Forum and Kamppi shopping centres, and even the
Academic Bookstore, without ever emerging above ground.

The two department stores and the Forum shopping centre
have their food stores on the subterranean level, which are better
places to look for typical foods than in the tourist shops. Browse
the shelves for wild-berry preserves and the coolers for smoked
fish and venison. Both departments stores have good sections for
Finnish design, in both fashion and home furnishings, as well as
sections for typical local products, including genuine Sámi-made
goods. The Kamppi shopping centre offers designer shops and a
variety of restaurants and cafés. If you feel adventurous take the

eastbound metro from the train station to Itäkeskus, where you'll find a huge shopping centre.

The underground routes access at least two of Helsinki's architectural landmarks, the interior of Eliel Saarinen's railway station and the Academic Bookstore, designed by Alvar Aalto. And close to their exits are two art museums well worth exploring on a rainy day: the Ateneum (see page 71), with the country's best collections of Finnish and foreign art, and Kiasma, the Museum of Contemporary Art (see page 74), featuring post-1960 Finnish works. (Without the visible landmarks of the world above, it is easy to lose your bearings in the tunnels, so signs help you find your way.)

🔽 *The Academic Bookstore is a destination in its own right*

On arrival

TIME DIFFERENCE

Helsinki follows Eastern European Time (EET), two hours ahead of GMT. During Daylight Saving Time (end Mar–end Oct) the clocks are put forward one hour.

ARRIVING

By air

Helsinki-Vantaa International Airport (**☎** 0200 14636
🌐 www.helsinki-vantaa.fi) is 19 km (12 miles) north of the city centre. The two-terminal (domestic and international) airport has three shopping centres and numerous bureaux de change and ATMs. Finnair operates a shuttle to Helsinki Railway Station, leaving every 20–30 minutes between 05.00–00.00 and costing €5.90 for the 30-minute journey. Public buses take around 40 minutes to reach the station but cost slightly less (€4) and depart every 10–30 minutes between 05.00–03.00. Taxis deliver you and your luggage directly to your hotel for about €40–45.

An alternative gateway used by low-cost airlines such as Ryanair is **Tampere-Pirkkala Airport** (**☎** 03 283 5311 **🌐** www.finavia.fi), usually known as Tampere. Bus timetables are linked to arrival times with the shuttles going direct to Helsinki Railway Station; the one-way fare is €25 and journey time 2½ hours.

By rail

Rail passengers arrive at one of Helsinki's great architectural landmarks, Eliel Saarinen's 1911 granite **Helsingin rautatieasema** (Helsinki Railway Station **ⓐ** Kaivokatu 1 **☎** 0600 41 900 **🌐** www.vr.fi). This busy terminus has a wealth of facilities – including restaurants and coffee shops, ATMs, public card phones and its own shopping centre – and is right in the centre of the city. Unlike many other large European stations, it is located in a busy, safe and upmarket area.

By road

Coach services arrive at the high-tech underground **Kamppi station** (ⓐ Narinkka 3 ⓣ 0200 4000 ⓦ www.matkahuolto.fi). Finnish buses and coaches are reliable and comfortable and get you to places where trains do not go.

In Helsinki, traffic is light, roads are well marked (and free of tolls) and drivers polite. But unless you plan to travel outside the capital and into the countryside, a car is really not necessary because public transport is so good.

If you are from a left-hand-drive country, be especially aware that in Finland driving is on the right, and cars overtake on the left. Drivers bringing their own cars from the UK should be sure their lights are adapted to right-hand driving. Drivers from outside the EU should carry an International Driving Permit (available from local automobile clubs before leaving home), along with their national licence. Unless otherwise posted, the speed limit is 80 kph (50 mph) outside the city, 50 kph (30 mph) within city limits and 100–120 kph (60–75 mph) on motorways (the limit increases with the number of lanes). In the city, trams, bicycles and pedestrians have right of way over cars. Seatbelts are compulsory everywhere.

If you intend to travel by car in the winter, you should be familiar with handling a vehicle on snow-covered and icy roads and driving in winter storm conditions. Winter wheels are mandatory in every car between November and March. Anywhere outside the city, be aware that reindeer and elk are formidable obstacles that can appear suddenly in the road at any time. Hundreds of people are

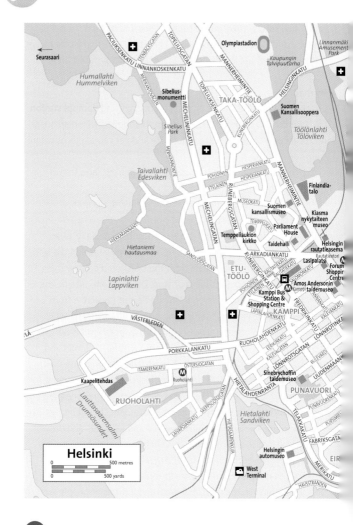

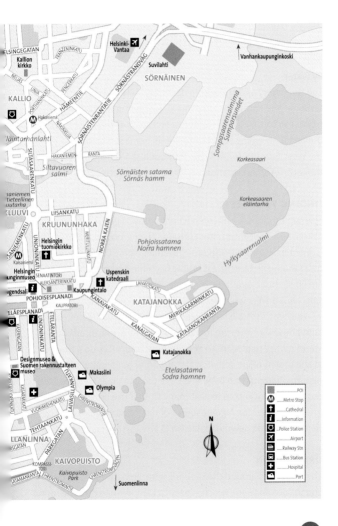

ELSINGEGATAN

Kallion
kirkko

Helsinki-✈
Vantaa

Suvilahti

Vanhankauruninkoski

SÖRNÄINEN

KALLIO

Ⓜ Hakaniemi

läintarhanlahti

HAKANIEMEN

RANTA

Siltavuoren
salmi

Sörnäisten satama
Sörnäs hamm

Korkeasaari

saniemen
tieteellinen
uutarha

Korkeasaaren
eläintarha

KLUUVI Ⓜ

LIISANKATU

KRUUNUNHAKA

Kaisaniemi

Pohjoissatama
Norra hamnen

Hylkysaarensalmi

Helsingin
tuomiokirkko ✝

Helsingin
unginmuseo

SENAATINTORI

ALEKSANTERINKATU

Uspenskin
katedraali

LAIVASTOKATU

igendsali ℹ

POHJOISESPLANADI

KAUPPATORI

Kaupungintalo

KATAJANOKKA

KANAVAKATU

MERIKASARMINKATU

KANALGATAN

KATAJANOKANRANTA

ELÄESPLANADI ℹ

ETELÄRANTA

Designmuseo &
Suomen rakennustaiteen
museo

Makasiini

Olympia

Katajanokka

Etelasatama
Sodra hamnen

TEHTAANKATU

N

LLÄNLINNA

KAIVOPUISTO

KOMPASSI-
TORI

Kaivopuisto
Park

Suomenlinna

🟥	POI
Ⓜ	Metro Stop
✝	Cathedral
ℹ	Information
▣	Police Station
✈	Airport
🚆	Railway Stn
🚌	Bus Station
✚	Hospital
⚓	Port

killed in wildlife collisions annually, so slow down whenever you see one, and be especially careful at dusk or in the dark.

By water

The three ferry and cruise ship docks, Olympia Terminal, Makasiini Terminal and Katajanokka Terminal, are right in the centre of the city in the South Harbour, within a few steps of the market, the Esplanadi, shopping streets and hotels. Some services arrive at the West Terminal in the West Harbour just a short bus ride from the centre. For information, see ⓦ www.portofhelsinki.fi.

FINDING YOUR FEET

Few capital cities are as compact or as easy to get around in as Helsinki. The central sites surround the harbour, and the city is laid out in a tidy grid with broad avenues. Some of Helsinki's most outstanding architecture is visible from the harbour, and its streets are lined with elegant old buildings. The city is clean, well lit and safe, with drivers who are careful of pedestrians.

The neat, sensible street plan makes finding addresses easy (and house numbers are marked on most local maps), although street names may seem to defy pronunciation. Pick up a free map at the tourist office, either at the airport or at Pohjoisesplanadi 19, near the harbour (see page 153). Here you can buy a Helsinki Card, economical if you plan to visit many sites or use public transport often (see page 58). A great source of neighbourhood maps is *See Helsinki on Foot*, downloadable via ⓦ www.visithelsinki.fi

ORIENTATION

The city wraps around the harbour, with Senaatintori (Senate Square, see page 70), which is easy to identify thanks to the round

IF YOU GET LOST, TRY ...

Excuse me, do you speak English?
Anteeksi, puhutko englantia?
Erntehksi, puhutko ehnglerntier?

How do I get to ...?
Miten mä pääsen ...?
Miten mah pa-a-sen ...?

Can you show me on my map?
Voitko näyttää mulle kartasta?
Voytko na-ewtta-a mulleh kerterster?

dome of the Lutheran Cathedral, behind it. To the east the golden
domes of Uspenski Cathedral (see page 70), on a second hill,
provide another useful landmark, and to the west stretches the
Esplanadi (see page 64), a wide park bordered by elegant buildings.
From the end of the Esplanadi, the broad Mannerheimintie heads
northwest, alongside the railway station and the bay of Toolonlahti.
Between those is the unmistakable Finlandia Hall (see page 73)
and a bit further up the Opera House (see page 75), with the
Parliament House (Ⓐ Mannerheiminte 30) and the tall tower
of the National Museum of Finland (see page 74) as landmarks
on Mannerheimintie's western side.

From this walkable nucleus, other neighbourhoods are easy
to find: the art nouveau Katajanokka beyond Uspenski Cathedral,
Kallio north of Senate Square, Sibelius Park and Hietaniemi to the

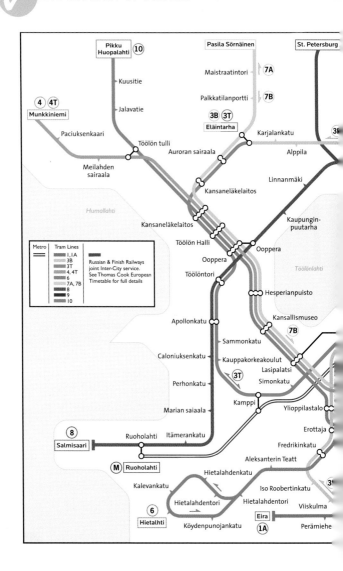

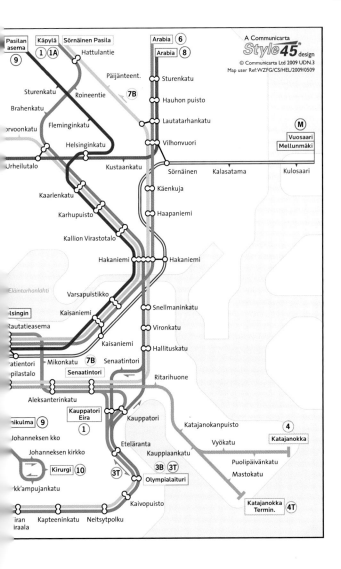

west, Bulevardi to its south and the neighbourhoods and parks of the southern end of the peninsula. The three main islands – Seurasaari, Suomenlinna and Korkeasaari – are respectively west, southeast and east of the city. The handy website Ⓦ http://kartta.hel.fi will help you locate any street address.

GETTING AROUND

Buses, trams and a single metro line make getting around Helsinki easy. The website Ⓦ http://journey.fi has a journey planner that gives you exact public transport connections between any two points, including scheduled times. Tickets can be purchased in advance from machines at stations and are valid on all forms of land-based transport in the city. If you expect to use public transport often, a tourist ticket allowing unlimited use of the system costs €6.80 for 24 hours, €13.60 for three days and €20.40 for five days. Otherwise, single tickets cost €2 and allow transfers within the hour. You can also buy a slightly cheaper tram-only single ticket for €1.80 (from machines). Bus drivers do sell single tickets, but these are more expensive at €2.50.

Another option is the Helsinki Card (one day €33, two days €45, three days €55), which also includes free admission to museums and attractions. This is only good value, however, if you plan to visit several attractions, since admission fees to most major sights are around €5–8. Entrance to all the separate museums on Suomenlinna plus the ferry trip adds up to more than a 24-hour Helsinki Card, but that assumes that you would tour every little museum in the complex.

Ferries shuttle continuously between the harbour and Suomenlinna (€3.80 return) and a little less frequently to Korkeasaari Zoo from the harbour or Hakaniemenranta.

Hail taxis from the street (the yellow sign will be lit if it is available), or at busy times go to a taxi rank or phone ☎ 0100 0700. The base rate is €5.10, or €8.00 at night and weekends. A journey to most city destinations will cost €7–11. Tipping is not necessary, but if you do, add €1 to the fare.

In good weather, consider cycling as a way to get between sights. The city is relatively flat and 900 km (over 500 miles) of cycle lanes and paths follow the major streets. Look for the free City Bikes in green racks, available for a €2 deposit.

If you're thinking of travelling further afield, you'll have to take a train, plane or coach. Getting around Finland is easy and efficient

Trams in central Helsinki

using buses, trains or internal flights, but it can be expensive unless you fall into one of the discount groups. The fastest trains are the Pendolinos, connecting major points, such as Helsinki and Turku. Express trains connect to northern cities, such as Rovaniemi, which is an 11-hour journey. InterRail, Eurail and other passes are valid in Finland (see page 143). Bus services are scheduled to be compatible with trains, reaching out into the countryside and smaller towns. Finnair flies to Rovaniemi and other points in the north.

Bus information ☎ 0200 4000 Ⓦ www.matkahuolto.fi
or the journey planner Ⓦ www.journey.fi
Finnair ☎ 0600 140 140 Ⓦ www.finnair.com
Train information ☎ 0600 41 902 Ⓦ www.vr.fi

CAR HIRE

All major companies are represented in Helsinki, most with desks at Helsinki-Vantaa Airport. Check car-hire rates before making air reservations, since you can often save with an air-car package from the airline.

If you plan to visit Helsinki before travelling elsewhere, consider picking up the car as you leave, instead of on arrival, to save city driving and parking charges. The minimum age for car hire is 18, and you must present (and carry while driving) your own home driver's licence. Non-EU residents should also have an International Driving Permit, obtained from an automobile club (you needn't be a member) before leaving home. In addition, you will need to show a credit card, even if you are not charging the car to one. If you plan to take the car on the ferry to Estonia or Sweden, be sure you have the necessary documentation (you should ask for this when you book).

▶ *Helsinki Railway Station*

THE CITY OF
Helsinki

Esplanadi & the Harbour

So many of Helsinki's most popular sights are in the streets surrounding the harbour that it would be easy to spend several days in this area without venturing any further. Outstanding architecture, churches, museums, dining and shopping are all within a few steps of the busy waterfront, which, given the number of ships and boats that seem to be constantly moving in and out, is itself a scenic attraction.

SIGHTS & ATTRACTIONS

Half the fun of visiting Helsinki is the variety of sights and experiences. High on that list is just ambling around the harbour and through the city's markets, enjoying the architecture and the constantly changing waterscape. Each time you approach the harbour, it looks different, as the huge Baltic ferries and cruise ships come and go, and little boats sail in and out.

Design District Helsinki

The area around Diana Park is full of design and antique shops, fashion stores, museums, art galleries, restaurants and showrooms. Here you can find fascinating examples of the work of the people who really matter. For an immediate immersion into the aesthetic that governs Finnish design, one could do a lot worse than pay a visit to this area. Guided walking tours of the Design District Helsinki are organised by the company Helsinki Expert (see page 36). Walks start from the Esplanade Park on Mondays and Fridays at 14.00. For an up-to-date list of participating venues and artists check
ⓦ www.designdistrict.fi

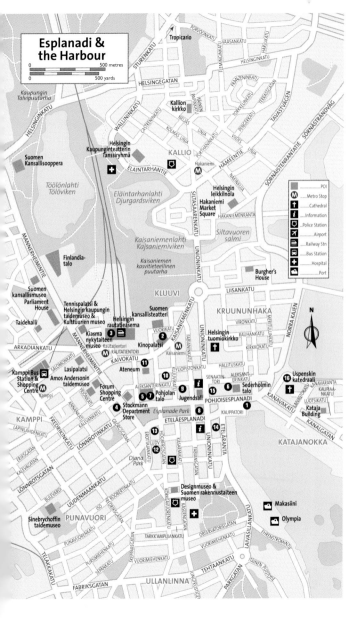

Esplanadi & the Harbour

| 0 | 500 metres |
| 0 | 500 yards |

Tropicario

Kaupungin Talvipuutarha

HELSINGINKATU

STURENKATU

PORVOONKATU

VAASANKATU

FLEMINGINKATU

HELSINGINKATU

HARJUKATU

HELSINGEGATAN

WALLININKATU

CASTRENINKATU

NELJÄS

KOLMAS LINJA

TOINEN LINJA

ENSI LINJA

PORTHANINKATU

JOSAFATINKATU

FRANZENINKATU

WILHELMSBERGINTIE

TORKKELINKATU

TERÄSKATU

TAVASTVÄGEN

Suomen Kansallisooppera

Helsingin Kaupunginteatterin tanssiryhmä

KALLIO

Kallion kirkko

ELÄINTARHANTIE

Hakaniemi

HÄMEENTIE

MÄKELÄNTIE

SÖRNÄISTENRANTATIE

SÖRNÄSTRANDVÄG

Töölönlahti Tölöviken

Finlandia-talo

Eläintarhanlahti Djurgårdsviken

SILTASAARENKATU

Helsingin leikkiluola

Hakaniemi Market Square

HAKANIEMENRANTA

Siltavuoren salmi

Kaisaniemenlahti Kajsaniemiviken

Kaisaniemen kasvitieteellinen puutarha

UNIONINKATU

Burgher's House

LIISANKATU

MANNERHEIMINTIE

Suomen kansallismuseo Parliament House

Taidehalli

Tennispalatsi & Helsingin kaupungin taidemuseo & Kulttuurien museo

Kiasma nykytaiteen museo

rautatientori

KLUUVI

Suomen kansallisteatteri

Helsingin rautatieasema

RAUTATIENTORI

VUORIKATU

KAISANIEMENKATU

FABIANINKATU

Kinopalatsi

Kaisaniemi

UNIONINKATU

KRUUNUNHAKA

VIRONKATU

RAUHANKATU

MERITULLINKATU

NORRA KAJEN

Helsingin tuomiokirkko

KIRKKOKATU

ARKADIANKATU

KAIVOKATU

Ateneum

KYLIÖPISTONKATU

HALLITUSKATU

SENAATIN-TORI

ALEKSAN-TERINK.

Kamppi Bus Station & Shopping Centre

Kamppi

Lasipalatsi

Amos Andersonin taidemuseo

SALOMONKATU

Forum Shopping Centre

Stockmann Department Store

ANNANKATU

KALEVANKATU

GEORGSGATAN

ALEKSANTERINKATU

Pohjolan talo

Jugendsali

Esplanade Park

ETELÄESPLANADI

POHJOISESPLANADI

Sederholmin talo

KAUPPATORI

Uspenskin katedraali

KANAVARANTA

KAUPPIAANKATU

LUOTSIKATU

Kataja Building

KANAVAKATU

KATAJANOKKA

KANALGATAN

KAMPPI

LAPINLAHDENKATU

FREDRIKINKATU

LÖNNROTINKATU

Diana Park

EROTTAJANKATU

HÖGBERGSGATAN

YRJÖNKATU

UNIONINKATU

FABIANINKATU

ETELÄRANTA

ERIKSGATAN

KALEVAGATAN

LÖNNROTSGATAN

BULEVARDI

UUDENMAANKATU

ISO ROOBERTINKATU

KORKEAVUORENKATU

Designmuseo & Suomen rakennustaiteen museo

KASARMINKATU

Makasiini

Olympia

Sinebrychoffin taidemuseo

PUNAVUORI

PUNAVUORENKATU

PURSIMIEHENKATU

SEPÄNKATU

SKEPPAREGATAN

TARKK'AMPUJANKATU

VUORIMIEHENKATU

OBSERVATORIEGATAN

VUORIMIEHENKATU

LAIVASILLANKATU

EHRENSTRÖMINTIE

TEHTAANKATU

TELAKKAKATU

FABRIKSGATAN

ULLANLINNA

PUISTOKATU

ITÄINEN

JUNGFRUSTIGEN

PARKGATAN

N

POI
M ....Metro Stop
Cathedral
i ....Information
Police Station
Airport
Railway Stn
Bus Station
Hospital
Port

1 2 3 4 5 6 7 8 9 10 11 12 13 14 15 16

Esplanadi

Stretching west from Kauppatori (Market Square), the open
swath of the Esplanadi is bordered by elegant buildings. Two
streets make up the Esplanadi, the Eteläesplanadi and, slightly
to the north, the Pohjoisesplanadi. The pavilion at the beginning
of the park is the Café Kappeli, and the nearby bandstand is the

ART NOUVEAU

At the turn of the 20th century, a unique combination of events,
ideas and talents propelled Finland and its capital city into the
spotlight of European design. Finland's rising intellectual and
artistic community, already seeking its own national identity
(see page 14), was further inspired by the Arts and Crafts
Movement popular in Europe at the time. Today, the results
of that Golden Age of Finnish Art make Helsinki a living
museum of art nouveau, or Jugendstil, as it was known
in German-speaking countries.

The primary architects were Lars Sonck, Sigurd Frosterus,
Selim Lindqvist, Valter Thomé, Herman Gesellius, Armas Lindgren
and Eliel Saarinen. Helsinki was in a rapid growth spurt, so housing
and public buildings were in great demand – and so were these
brilliant young architects to design them. Dozens of their
landmark buildings cluster in easy-to-visit neighbourhoods.

One of Europe's signature buildings in this style is Saarinen's
Helsinki Railway Station, whose dramatic straight lines are
accented by stylised figures holding lamps. The interior is a
triumph of art nouveau, combining elegantly simple structure

scene of free summer concerts. Before Christmas, the entire Esplanadi is lined with booths selling crafts and food. Between it and Market Square, a statue of Helsinki's symbol, Havis Amanda, emerges from a fountain. The fountain is the work of Eliel Saarinen, and Havis Amanda is by Ville Vallgren. Esplanade Park, between the two streets, is filled with strollers on summer evenings.

with flowing lines of natural ornamental designs.

In the nearby downtown streets are several other noteworthy structures; one of the most outstanding is the Pohjola Insurance Building at Aleksanterinkatu 44 (see page 68). You can't miss its rusticated stone exterior, and its interior mixes stone with the local wood, using designs of local plants and animals. Climb the curving stairs to see art nouveau balustrades, doors, hinges, panels, even the newel post.

Just beyond the Uspenski Cathedral (see page 70) are some of the city's best residential examples. Katajanokka (see page 67) was the first neighbourhood of this type in Europe, and is also Europe's best preserved. Walk along the streets of this five-block quarter, looking for details of stone ornament as well as surprising doorways, fanciful hinges, fairytale towers, balconies and other architectural details.

To see the best of Helsinki's art nouveau, sign up for the 'Pearls of Jugend' tour with Archtours. Architect Marianna Heikinheimo or one of her associates will take you to the best art nouveau neighbourhoods and hard-to-reach out-of-town sites. **Archtours** ❶ 09 4777 300 Ⓦ www.archtours.fi

Helsingin leikkiluola (Helsinki Playground)

A great place for families on a rainy day. You have two hours
(🕐 10.00–12.00, 12.00–14.00 up to 18.00–20.00) to make full use of
the bouncy castles, trampolines and Lego. There's enough to go round
for all the kids, large and small. 🅰 Jaffa Station, Sörnäisten rantatie 6,
at Hakaniemi Market Square 🕐 020 710 9902 🕸 www.leikkiluola.fi
🕐 10.00–20.00 🅽 Metro: Hakaniemi; tram: 1A, 3B, 6, 7B, 8, 9.
Admission charge for children, parents free

Helsingin rautatieasema (Helsinki Railway Station)

For visitors arriving by rail or airport bus, the first stop is Helsinki's
art nouveau railway station, designed by Eliel Saarinen. Its tower is
said to have influenced America's first generation of skyscrapers,
including the 1929 Gulf Building in Houston, Texas, now owned
by JPMorgan Chase. Be sure to go inside to see the monumental
arched halls, with walls decorated with surprisingly delicate carved
panels. 🅰 Rautatientori 🅽 Metro: Rautatientori

Jugendsali (Jugend Hall)

Jugendstil meets medieval in this 1904 interior by architect Lars Sonck.
Romanesque churches seem to inspire the banking hall's low vaulting
and three 'naves', but the similarities end there. Sonck uses the stone
itself as a decorative material, sometimes rough-surfaced and
rusticated, or polished to a high gloss in the muscular pillars. Relief
carvings in their capitals are reminiscent of Viking ship prows, a popular
Scandinavian theme but not frequently seen in Finland. Today, the hall
serves as a café and hosts the occasional concert and art exhibition
as well. 🅰 Pohjoisesplanadi 19 🕐 09 3101 3800 🕐 09.00–17.00
Mon–Fri, 11.00–17.00 Sun, Aug–June; 09.00–16.00 Mon–Fri, July
🅽 Tram: 1A, 3T

Kaisaniemen kasvitieteellinen puutarha (Kaisaniemi Botanical Gardens)

The iron-framed glass Palm House was designed by Gustaf Nystrom in 1889, and today more than 900 labelled plant species grow in rainforest, desert, Mediterranean and water environments. Go in the winter to be among orchids, African violets and water lilies with massive leaves. The flowerbeds, fountains, pools and rose borders are beautiful in June. ⓐ Enter from Unioninkatu 44 or Kaisaniemenranta 2, near the railway station ⓣ 09 1912 4453 ⓛ Gardens: 09.00–20.00 Apr–Sept; 09.00–17.00 Oct–Mar; glasshouses: 10.00–17.00 Tues–Sun, Apr–Sept; 10.00–15.00 Tues–Sun, Oct–Mar. Admission charge to glasshouses

Kallion kirkko (Kallio Church)

One of Finland's great architects, Lars Sonck, designed this great church in the National Romantic style in 1912. The bells inside its distinctive tower play a piece by Sibelius. Go inside the granite building to see the sculpted relief and other works of art, and go for a Sunday service or a concert to hear the great organs. ⓐ Itäinen Papinkatu 2 ⓣ 09 2340 3620 ⓛ 12.00–17.00 Mon–Fri, 10.00–18.00 Sat & Sun ⓝ Tram: 1A, 3B, 9

Katajanokka

The city's best concentration of art nouveau architecture can be found in the streets beyond Uspenski Cathedral, across the harbour from Kauppatori (Market Square). Built within a decade, at the height of Jugendstil's popularity, this is Europe's best preserved art nouveau residential neighbourhood. Each new apartment building, for the wealthy middle class who could afford quality design and construction, was designed to outdo its neighbours. The castle-like Aeolus building and the turreted Tallbergin Talo, across the street, form a gate to the quarter, at either side of Luotsikatu, which is lined with fine examples. Behind Tallbergin is another signature building, Eol, with a projecting balcony, corner turret and outstanding wooden door with elegant iron fittings and carved mythic creatures. The most exquisite doorway, however, is on the 1902 **Kataja building** (ⓐ Kaupiaankatu 2 Ⓝ Tram: 4T).

Kauppatori (Market Square)
At the harbour's edge, with some of its merchants selling directly from boats, is the colourful market, a daily gathering of locals, visitors, farmers, fishermen, craftsmen and traders. Impromptu cafés, enclosed by plastic in the winter, serve everything from juicy sausages to salmon fillets grilled on cedar planks. At the Esplanadi side of the harbour is Gustaf Nystrom's 1889 market, worth visiting for the market stalls of honey, smoked fish, local cheese and other delicacies. ⓐ Helsinki Harbour Ⓛ Indoor market: 08.00–18.00 Mon–Fri, 08.00–16.00 Sat; outdoor market: 06.30–18.00 Mon–Fri, 06.30–16.00 Sat (also 10.00–17.00 Sun in summer) Ⓝ Tram: 1A, 3T

Pohjolan talo (Pohjola Insurance Building)
The interior motifs used in this 1901 office building by Saarinen, Lindgren & Gesellius are clearly Finnish, but the style shows the influence of French art nouveau. The dramatic sweeping staircase is asymmetrical, bordered in graceful balustrades. Art nouveau elements decorate these, as well as the walls and doorways of each landing. To see the interior, go during weekday business hours, wait until someone opens the door and simply walk in. ⓐ Aleksanterinkatu 44 Ⓝ Tram: 3B, 3T, 4T, 7A/B

Ⓞ *Katajanokka is an outdoor museum of art nouveau domestic architecture*

THE CITY

Senaatintori & tuomiokirkko (Senate Square & Lutheran Cathedral)

Up the hill behind the market, its dome visible above the row of
intervening buildings, the majestic neoclassical Lutheran Cathedral
is the focal point of Senate Square. The buildings at its adjoining
sides, also by C L Engel, create an unusually unified public space –
and one of Europe's finest squares. It's a well used one, too, for
celebrations that range from Finland's Independence Day to the
start of the St Lucia Parade before Christmas. The early 19th-century
cathedral, with its tall green dome, stands high above the square,
at the top of a long flight of steps. Sederholm House, the oldest
stone building in Helsinki, faces the lower corner of the square.
ⓐ Intersection of Unioninkatu and Aleksanterinkatu streets
ⓣ 09 2340 6120 ⓒ Cathedral: 09.00–00.00 summer; 09.00–18.00
winter ⓝ Tram: 1A, 3T, 4T, 7A/B

Tropicario

This is the most modern and exciting tropical terrarium in
Scandinavia. It boasts fantastic examples of some amazing flora
and fauna, including crocs, snakes and lizards of all types, with which
you can interact up close and personal. This plot of Finnish jungle
really isn't one for the phobic, but everybody else will have a roaring
good time. ⓐ Sturenkatu 27 ⓣ 09 750 076 ⓦ www.tropicario.com
ⓒ 10.00–19.00 ⓝ Tram: 1A, 7B

Uspenskin katedraali (Uspenski Cathedral)

Dominating the far side of the harbour is western Europe's largest
Orthodox church, an ornate brick pile whose dome and towers are
crowned by 13 gold cupolas. The interior is a wondrous cavern of
icons, crosses, altars and gleaming gold, its intricately decorated
arches offset by black marble columns. Along with serving the

local Orthodox and Russian population, the church marks Helsinki's long-standing Russian influence. ⓐ Kanavakatu 1 ⓣ 020 7220 683 ⓛ 09.30–16.00 Mon–Fri, 09.30–14.00 Sat, 12.00–15.00 Sun, May–Sept; 09.30–16.00 Tues–Fri, 09.30–14.00 Sat, 12.00–15.00 Sun, Oct–Apr ⓝ Tram: 4T

CULTURE

A high concentration of the city's many museums lies in this central area; all are within easy walking distance of each other. The Helsinki Card admits visitors to nearly all of these, as well as to other attractions.

Amos Andersonin taidemuseo (Amos Anderson Art Museum)

This features mainly 20th-century Finnish art and furnishings from Amos Anderson's private collections. There is also Finnish and foreign art from the collection of the architect Sigurd Frosterus. As one would expect, both exhibit excellent taste. Watch out for special exhibitions. ⓐ Yrjönkatu 27 ⓣ 09 684 4460 ⓦ www.amosanderson.fi ⓛ 10.00–18.00 Mon, Thur & Fri, 10.00–20.00 Wed, 11.00–17.00 Sat & Sun ⓝ Metro: Rautatientori; tram: 3T. Admission charge

Ateneum

The building is a beautiful setting for Finnish painting, sculpture, graphics and drawings, as well as international art. Internationally it is strong in works from the 19th and early 20th centuries, including those of Gauguin, Modigliani and Degas. ⓐ Kaivokatu 2 (opposite railway station) ⓣ 09 1733 6401 ⓦ www.ateneum.fi ⓛ 10.00–18.00 Tues, Fri, 10.00–20.00 Wed & Thur, 11.00–17.00 Sat & Sun ⓝ Metro: Rautatientori. Admission charge

Designmuseo (Design Museum)

Nowhere is the evolution of decorative styles better illustrated
than in the ground-floor gallery of this Design Museum. Decorative
arts in ceramics, glass, metal, fabrics, furniture, utensils, and décor
show how various style periods interpreted these items. So if you are
unclear just how Victorian gave way to art nouveau and how that
morphed into art deco and modernism, you can see side-by-side
examples. Although the primary focus is on Finnish design, special
exhibitions may feature other designers or themes. The shop is a
treasure box of quality design gifts and books. ⓐ Korkeavuorenkatu 23
ⓣ 09 622 0540 ⓦ www.designmuseo.fi ⓒ 11.00–20.00 June–Aug;
11.00–20.00 Tues, 11.00–18.00 Wed–Sun, Sept–May ⓥ Tram: 10; bus:
16. Admission charge

◆ *Finlandia Hall is home to the Helsinki Philharmonic Orchestra*

Finlandia-talo (Finlandia Hall)

Famed architect Alvar Aalto's best-known work in Helsinki is the enormous concert hall overlooking Töölö Bay. It's no accident that its white Carrara marble and black granite remind you of a piano keyboard. Tours of the 1970s building are given when the hall is not in use. The hall is currently home to both the Helsingin kaupunginorkesteri (Helsinki Philharmonic Orchestra) and the Radion sinfoniaorkesteri (Radio Symphony Orchestra). These two excellent orchestras will move to the brand new **Helsinki Music Centre** (ⓦ www.musiikkitalo.fi) opposite the Parliament House when it opens in 2011. ⓐ Mannerheimintie 13 E ⓣ 09 402 41 ⓦ www.finlandiatalo.fi ⓛ Box office & visits: 07.30–17.00 Mon–Fri; performance times vary ⓜ Tram: 4, 4T, 7A, 7B, 10. Admission charge for tours

Helsingin kaupunginteatterin tanssiryhmä (Helsinki Contemporary Dance Theatre)

Finland's largest modern dance ensemble, with a busy programme of performances. ⓐ Elaintarhantie 5 in Hakaniemi, across Elaintarha north of the railway station ⓣ 09 394 022 ⓦ www.hkt.fi ⓛ Box office: 09.00–18.00 Mon–Fri ⓜ Metro: Hakaniemi; tram: 1A, 3B, 6, 7, 9. Tickets also available from ⓐ Eerikinkatu 2 ⓛ 09.00–19.00 Mon–Fri, 12.00–19.00 Sat

Kiasma nykytaiteen museo (Kiasma Museum of Contemporary Art)

The home of Finnish modern art is, like the city's other art museums, as much about the building as its contents. Designed by the American architect Steven Holl, the curvy Kiasma opened in 1998, and is considered one of Finland's paramount works of modern architecture – no small feat in the native land of so many well-known architects. It contains a theatre for experimental drama, dance and music, as well as collections of post-1960 Finnish art. ⓐ Mannerheiminaukio 2 ⓣ 09 173 36501 ⓦ www.kiasma.fi ⓛ 10.00–17.00 Tues, 10.00–20.30 Wed–Fri, 10.00–18.00 Sat & Sun ⓜ Metro: Rautatientori; tram: 4T, 7, 10. Admission charge

Sederholmin talo (Sederholm House)

Overlooking Senate Square, this is the central city's oldest stone building (built in 1757). It contains exhibitions from various city museums. ⓐ Aleksanterinkatu 16–18 ⓣ 09 3103 6529 ⓛ 11.00–17.00 Wed–Sun ⓜ Bus/tram: 1, 3T, 3B, 4. Admission charge

Suomen kansallismuseo (National Museum of Finland)

Your first stop to learn about Finnish culture and traditions, the museum also covers Finland's history from prehistoric to the present.

Historical artefacts and ethnographic collections illustrate daily life as well as events. Like the Ateneum, the building itself is a landmark, designed by the pre-eminent firm of Saarinen, Lindgren & Gesellius in 1902. 🄰 Mannerheimintie 34 🄣 09 4050 9544 🅆 www.nba.fi 🄻 11.00–20.00 Tues & Wed, 11.00–18.00 Thur–Sun 🄽 Bus/tram: 4, 4T, 7, 10. Admission charge

Suomen kansallisooppera (National Opera)

This modern stage is among Europe's finest, with revolving floor, flexible mirrored ceiling and other techno tricks. Behind-the-scene tours are offered on Wednesdays at 14.30, but are only given in Finnish. Tickets begin as low as €12, and some performances are free. As well as offering around a dozen opera productions a year, the theatre hosts performances by the Suomen kansallisbaletti (National Ballet). 🄰 Helsinginkatu 58 🄣 09 4030 21 🅆 www.operafin.fi 🄻 Box office: 09.00–18.00 Mon–Fri, 15.00–18.00 Sat 🄽 Tram: 3T, 4T, 7, 8, 10

Suomen kansallisteatteri (National Theatre)

The focal point of the north side of the Helsinki Railway Station Square is the National Theatre, built in 1902. The façade is in granite and sandstone, while the interior is almost entirely worked in curved lines. The foyer is decorated with frescoes. 🄰 Suomen Kansallisteatteri, Läntinen Teatterikuja 1 🅆 www.kansallisteatteri.fi 🄽 Metro: Rautatientori

Suomen rakennustaiteen museo (Museum of Finnish Architecture)

Special exhibitions highlight Finnish architects past and present, as well as the styles they created and influenced. 🄰 Kasarmikatu 24 🄣 09 8567 5100 🅆 www.mfa.fi 🄻 10.00–16.00 Tues, Thur & Fri, 10.00–20.00 Wed, 11.00–16.00 Sat & Sun 🄽 Tram: 10; bus: 16. Admission charge

CHRISTMAS MARKETS

Every Finnish school child knows that Santa lives in Finland,
just south of Rovaniemi, near the Arctic Circle. Many have
visited him there. The village where he lives with his elves and
reindeer, is open all year, except 24 December, but you don't
have to go all the way to the Arctic Circle to find the Finns
celebrating the Christmas season.

It begins early in December with the Christmas market
that springs up like a little village on the Esplanadi. Helsinki's
St Thomas Market forms a double row of bright tents, each
outlined in tiny twinkling white lights. Step inside each one to
find a tiny, brightly lit shop filled with beautiful handmade gifts:
woodcarvings, knitted hats and mittens, gingerbread, wrought
ironwork, fanciful candles, woven scarves, wooden toys, fur
hats, blown glass or jars of shimmering lingonberry jelly.

RETAIL THERAPY

The Esplanadi and the streets north – Mannerheimintie,
Aleksanterinkatu and Kaisaniemenkatu – are lined with the
smartest shops, featuring the best in Finnish design. Just browsing
their stunningly arranged windows is an art experience. On Senate
Square and the streets around it you will find boutiques selling
handicrafts and folk arts. In good weather, Market Square is filled
with stalls of crafts and other local goods. You could shop till you
drop without leaving this small area of Helsinki – take trams 4, 6,
7A/B, 9 or 10 to get here and then explore on foot.

Brightly painted wooden puzzles come in shapes of fish, turtles, rabbits and hedgehogs. Velvet-smooth wooden cooking utensils – spatulas, forks, spoons and spreaders – are carved in graceful flowing shapes, from richly grained woods. Cups are formed from the gnarly-grained tree burls and cutting boards show off a variety of local woods in contrasting stripes. More rustic are the Christmas elves made of small angle-cut logs, with beards of curly yarn and peaked caps of bright felt. Smaller elves of wool perch everywhere.

A warmer venue for a craft show is the **Women's Christmas Fair**, at the Wanha Satama, across Helsinki's harbour (🕐 10.00–19.00, 2–6 Dec 🚊 Tram: 4, 4T). The variety is astonishing, from stacks of beeswax candles and creamy Finnish honey to elegant painted silks, hobby-horses, finger puppets, fashionable knitwear and cheery little red-hatted elves, all created by Finnish women.

Aarikka Finland Clever, irresistible creations from wood include Christmas decorations, home décor, jewellery and whimsical utensils. 🅰 Pohjoisesplanadi 27 🌐 www.aarikka.fi 🕐 10.00–19.00 Mon–Fri, 10.00–17.00 Sat

Artek Furniture designed by Alvar Aalto forms the centrepiece, with other interior décor including rugs, linens, decorative fabrics and tableware. 🅰 Eteläesplanadi 18 ☎ 09 6132 5277 🕐 10.00–18.00 Mon–Fri, 10.00–16.00 Sat

Design Forum To see – and buy – what's new and hot, shop at Design Forum, where useful items from notebooks to kitchen appliances are practical, as well as beautiful and stylish, proving that Finnish design isn't just another pretty face. ⓐ Erottajankatu 7 ⓣ 09 6220 8130 ⓦ www.designforum.fi ⓛ 10.00–19.00 Mon–Fri, 12.00–17.00 Sat & Sun ⓝ Tram: 9, 10

🔺 *The Design Forum is Finland's shop window to the world*

Designers Gallery This is the place to be inspired by top quality modern fashion for women as envisaged by prize-winning Finnish designers such as Iris Aalto, Ilona Pelli and Tarja Niskanen ⓐ Kauppatori, Eteläesplanadi 4/Unioninkatu 26 ⓣ 050 340 8290 ⓛ 10.00–18.00 Mon–Fri, 10.00–16.00 Sat ⓜ Tram: 1A, 3T

Hakaniemi Market Hall Textiles and handicrafts fill the small shops on the upper floor above the food hall. A daily open-air market lines the square outside. ⓐ Hakaniemi ⓦ www.hakaniemenkauppahalli.fi ⓛ 08.00–18.00 Mon–Fri, 08.00–16.00 Sat ⓜ Metro: Hakaniemi; tram: 1, 3B, 6, 7, 9; bus: 23, 65, 66

Marimekko Famed for striking decorator fabrics, Marimekko also leads the design world with tableware, bags and wearables. ⓐ Various locations: Pohjoisesplanadi 2 & 31; Kamppi shopping centre; Urho Kekkosen katu 1 ⓣ 010 344 3300 ⓦ www.marimekko.com ⓛ Variable, so phone to check

Sokos Slightly less rarified than Stockmann, but with a wide variety of high-quality Finnish and Scandinavian goods, from fashions to furnishings, Sokos is near the railway station. ⓐ Mannerheimintie 9 ⓣ 010 766 5100 ⓛ 09.00–21.00 Mon–Fri, 09.00–18.00 Sat (also open 12.00–21.00 Sun, summer & Dec)

Stockmann Even an entire city block, extended in 2010, can't hold all the merchandise in the largest department store in the Nordic countries. The stock overflows into the Academic Bookstore, across Keskuskatu (and connected by a tunnel), in a building designed by Alvar Aalto. ⓐ Corner of Aleksanterinkatu and Mannerheimintie

W www.stockmann.fi ⏱ 09.00–21.00 Mon–Fri, 09.00–18.00 Sat
(also open 12.00–18.00 Sun, summer & Dec)

TAKING A BREAK

Central Helsinki is filled with cafés, from elegant Old World settings
to cafés in shops, museums and even a ship in the harbour. In the
summer many of them move outdoors to enjoy the long daylight hours.

Kauppatorin Kahvila £ ❶ In a bright orange tent in the market, but
warm inside even on blustery snow-filled days, this is a favourite
of local politicos, who come for the coffee and the outstanding meat
pies. 🅐 Kauppatori ☎ No phone W www.toripojat.fi ⏱ 06.00–14.00
Mon–Fri, 06.00–16.00 Sat, 08.00–16.00 Sun 🅝 Tram: 1, 3T, 4T, 7

Kipinä £ ❷ Unreserved atmosphere, cosy interior, excellent
homemade food and the friendly and professional service will
guarantee an unforgettable time. 🅐 Vuorikatu 16 ☎ 09 670 089
W www.marcante.fi/kipina ⏱ 11.00–00.00 Mon–Wed, 11.00–02.00
Thur–Fri, 15.00–02.00 Sat 🅝 Tram: 3B, 6, 9

Restaurant Eliel £ ❸ You might not choose a railway station for
a meal, but this café is very popular with locals and visitors for
good food and low prices. Breakfast is served until late morning,
the buffet lunch until late afternoon; there's a full evening menu.
🅐 Rautatieasema ☎ 040 862 2965 ⏱ 07.30–23.00 Mon–Fri,
08.00–23.00 Sat, 10.00–22.00 Sun 🅝 Metro: Rautatientori

Baker's Bar & Restaurant ££ ❹ Baker's is a versatile restaurant
complex in the heart of Helsinki. On the international menu you'll

find seasonal specialities as well as Finnish classics. During the week, a delicious buffet lunch is set from 11.00 till 14.00. A mouthwatering selection of different kinds of breads awaits all the gourmets. ⓐ Mannerheimintie 12 ⓣ 020 770 1440 ⓦ www.ravintolabakers.com ⓛ 11.00–22.00 Mon & Tues, 11.00–23.00 Wed–Fri, 13.00–23.00 Sat; café bar: 07.00–04.00 Mon–Fri, 10.00–04.00 Sat, 19.00–04.00 Sun ⓝ Tram: 3B, 4T, 6, 8, 9, 10

Café Aalto ££ ❺ On the balcony of the Academic Bookstore, the café overlooks the interior designed by Finnish design-meister Alvar Aalto. Relax with a book over coffee or have lunch here. The pastries are baked in-house. ⓐ Pohjoisesplanadi 39 ⓣ 09 121 4446 ⓦ www.cafeaalto.fi ⓛ 09.00–21.00 Mon–Fri, 09.00–18.00 Sat (also open 12.00–18.00 Sun, summer & Dec) ⓝ Tram: 3B, 3T, 4T, 6, 7, 9, 10

Café Engel ££ ❻ In the dark days of a northern winter, this cheering café is brightly illuminated with 'daylight' bulbs. The coffee menu is long and the lingonberry pie is mouthwatering. ⓐ Aleksanterinkatu 26 ⓣ 09 652 776 ⓦ www.cafeengel.fi ⓛ 08.00–22.00 Mon–Fri, 09.00–22.00 Sat, 10.00–22.00 Sun ⓝ Tram: 1A, 3T, 4, 7

Café Esplanad ££ ❼ You'd expect high prices at this Esplanadi terrace, but the sandwiches, pastries, soups and salads are quite reasonable. Add occasional live jazz performances and it's no wonder the place is so popular. Minimum age is 20 in the evenings. ⓐ Pohjoisesplanadi 37 ⓣ 09 665 496 ⓦ www.esplanad.fi ⓛ 08.00–22.00 Mon–Fri, 09.00–22.00 Sat, 10.00–22.00 Sun ⓝ Tram: 3B, 3T, 4, 6, 7, 9, 10

Café Kappeli ££ ❽ The café serves a soup lunch daily while the restaurant offers Finnish classics. Or you can just have a drink

● *Café Kappeli – a landmark on the Esplanadi*

at the bar. ⓐ Eteläesplanadi 1 ☎ 010 76 63880 ⓦ www.kappeli.fi
🕐 10.00–00.00 Ⓝ Tram: 1A, 3T, 4, 7

Karl Fazer Cafe ££ ❾ The venerable Fazer specialises in stunning
sweet delicacies but a selection of soups, salads and pasta is also
available at lunchtimes. The breakfast buffet is the best in town
and the desserts and chocolates are peerless. ⓐ Kluuvikatu 3
☎ 020 729 6702 ⓦ www.fazer.fi 🕐 07.30–22.00 Mon–Fri,
09.00–22.00 Sat Ⓝ Metro: Kaisaniemi; tram: 3T, 4T, 7

Memphis ££ ❿ This venue presents a hotch-potch of cuisines that's
rather too complex to be termed as fusion: the major influences are
Indian, American and Latin, and it's the skill with which they're combined
that really makes everything work. ⓐ Kluuvikatu 8 ☎ 09 4332 6310
ⓦ www.memphis.fi 🕐 11.00–00.00 Mon–Thur, 11.00–01.00 Fri,

12.00–10.00 Sat, 13.00–00.00 Sun ● Metro: Kaisaniemi; tram: 3B, 3T, 6, 7, 9

Tablo Ateneum ££ ⑪ The café in the Ateneum museum has a daily changing lunch menu along with soups, pastries and cakes. ⓐ Rautatientori ● 09 1733 6231 ● 10.00–17.30 Tues & Fri, 11.00–19.30 Wed & Thur, 11.00–16.30 Sat & Sun ● Metro: Rautatientori; tram: 3B, 3T, 6, 9

AFTER DARK

Friday and Saturday are the big nights for partying, but Wednesday is also popular for clubs. Book ahead for dinner at the more sought after restaurants in the city centre at weekends or in the summer.

RESTAURANTS

Rymy-Eetu ££ ⑫ An ongoing Oktoberfest in the centre of Helsinki. Alongside its full menu, Rymy-Eetu serves breakfast until 18.00 and a retro-style lunch at midday. A wide selection of beers will keep you going in between and there's live music almost every night. ⓐ Erottajankatu 15–17 ● 09 670 310 ● 11.00–03.00, Mon & Tues, 11.00–04.00 Wed–Sat ● Tram: 3B, 6, 9, 10

Vespa ££ ⑬ Three Italian restaurants in one: a delicious upstairs ristorante, a busy street-level bar and deli and an atmospheric cellar trattoria. ⓐ Eteläesplanadi 22 ● 020 7701 460 ● www.ravintolavespa.fi ● Ristorante: 11.00–23.00 Mon, 11.00–00.00 Tues–Fri, 13.00–23.00 Sat; bar & deli: 08.00–23.00 Mon, 08.00–00.00 Tues–Thur, 08.00–01.00 Fri, 13.00–01.00 Sat; trattoria: 17.00–00.00 Tues–Sat ● Tram: 3B, 6, 9, 10

83

G W Sundmans £££ ⓮ One of Finland's oldest restaurants, and still one of its best, Sundmans occupies a beautifully restored former mansion. Art nouveau interior details are soon forgotten as the food arrives, from the heavenly terrines with woodland mushrooms to the dessert of Arctic cloudberries. ⓐ Eteläranta 16 (facing the harbour) ⓣ 09 6128 5400 ⓦ www.royalravintolat.com/sundmans ⓛ 11.00–14.30, 17.00–00.00 Mon–Fri, 18.00–00.00 Sat ⓝ Tram: 4, 7B

Sasso £££ ⓯ From the smart, stylish doorway on Market Square to the stunning presentation, Sasso combines Italian cooking with Finnish design. It's a happy mixture, and the food is always paramount, as Nordic ingredients join imported Italian. ⓐ Pohjoisesplanadi 17 ⓣ 09 1345 6240 ⓦ www.palacekamp.fi ⓛ 11.30–15.00, 17.00–23.00 Mon & Tues, 11.30–15.00, 17.00–00.00 Wed–Sat ⓝ Tram: 1, 3T, 4T, 7

Sipuli £££ ⓰ The skylight looks straight up at the domes of Uspenski Cathedral. Nordic ingredients from the sea and forest are elegantly prepared – a frothy pumpkin soup is sprinkled with roasted nuts, and fried scallops are paired with fennel purée and pomegranate vinaigrette. ⓐ Kanavaranta 7 ⓣ 09 6128 5500 ⓦ www.royalravintolat.com/sipuli ⓛ 18.00–00.00 Mon–Fri ⓝ Tram 4T; bus 16

BARS & CLUBS
Gaselli Patrons here can enjoy an extensive range of tapped beers and over 40 bottled products. Finnish pop and rock is often played in this relaxed venue, but don't let that put you off. ⓐ Aleksanterinkatu 46 ⓣ 09 8568 5760 ⓦ www.rafla.fi/pubgaselli ⓛ 16.00–02.00 Tues–Thur, 16.00–03.00 Fri, 18.00–03.00 Sat ⓝ Tram: 3T, 4T, 7

Hotel Kämp With around 100 varieties of wine sold by the glass, the bar in Hotel Kämp (see page 40) is the classiest place in town for a drink. Prices are surprisingly reasonable and there's a good brasserie and Japanese restaurant on-site as well. ③ Pohjoisesplanadi 29 ① 09 576 1111 ⊙ 10.00–01.00 Mon–Wed, 10.00–02.00 Tues–Fri, 11.00–02.00 Sat, 11.00–01.00 Sun ⊙ Metro: Kaisaniemi

Mecca This joint positively exudes soul, and the vast selection of cocktails only helps this spiritual dimension. There's a DJ from Wednesday to Saturday. ③ Korkeavuorenkatu 34 ① 09 1345 6200 ⓦ www.mecca.fi ⊙ 17.00–00.00 Tues–Thur, 17.00–04.00 Fri & Sat; kitchen: 18.00–22.00 Tues–Sat ⊙ Tram: 9, 10; bus 42

Redrum Name the type of music that gets you going and you'll find it in this wood-panelled club that boasts superb acoustics and a nifty sound system by Funktion-One. ③ Vuorikatu 2 ⓦ www.redrum.fi ⊙ 22.00–04.00 ⊙ Tram: 3B, 3T, 4T, 6, 7, 9

CINEMA & ENTERTAINMENT

Kinopalatsi For American mainstream and occasional European films, check the ten screens at this multi-level cinema complex near the railway station. Tickets are discounted for weekday matinées. Cafés, Wi-Fi, shops and game arcades complete the centre. ③ Kaisaniemenkatu 2 ① 0600 007 007 ⓦ www.kinopalatsi.fi ⊙ From 11.00 ⊙ Metro: Kaisaniemi; tram: 3B, 6, 9

Lasipalatsi A multi-purpose entertainment, film and media centre, offering Wi-Fi access, numerous cafés and restaurants, a library, frequent exhibitions and screenings of European cinema. ③ Mannerheimintie 22–24 ① 09 6126 570 ⓦ www.lasipalatsi.fi ⊙ Metro: Rautatientori; tram: 4, 7, 10

Western & northern Helsinki

The broad Mannerheimintie slices the part of Helsinki lying north of the Esplanadi neatly in half. Although it may seem as though everything you could want is on the harbour (eastern) side of that line, there is a lot more to see if you cross it. Fewer museums and attractions, perhaps, but more of the city's colourful nightlife and a great deal of its shopping lie in the streets adjoining Uudenmankatu, Lönnrotinkatu and the shopping street of Frederikinkatu. Some of the city's most frequently visited attractions are in this area. Among these are the Temppeliaukio Church (Church in the Rock), the Olympic Stadium and Linnanmäki, Finland's most popular amusement park.

SIGHTS & ATTRACTIONS

Hietaniemen hautausmaa (Hietaniemi Cemetery)

On All Saints, Christmas and Independence Day, Finns visit cemeteries not only to remember loved ones, but also to honour national heroes and those fallen in wars. Along with the public observations, it's a personal thing with many Finns to remember those who died for their country or who contributed to culture or public life. Hietaniemi is especially busy on 6 December, Independence Day, when the march of students to Senate Square begins here. Buried in its elegant park setting, along with a clutch of presidents in Statesman's Grove, is Marshal Mannerheim, Commander-in-chief of Finnish forces in World War II after the Soviet attack on Finland in 1939. Architects Alvar Aalto and Engel, and artist Albert Edelfelt rest on Artists Hill.
ⓐ Mechelininkatu Ⓝ Tram: 8; bus: 15A

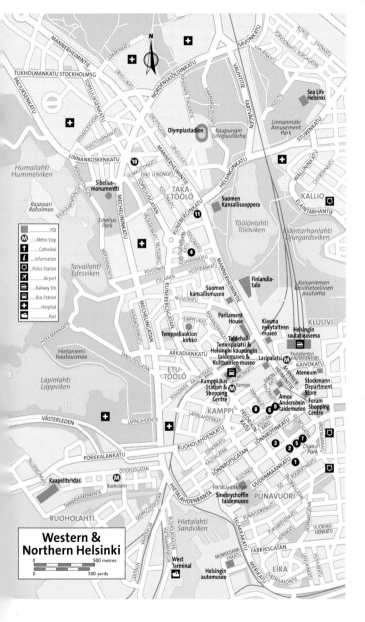

Western & Northern Helsinki

0   500 metres
0   500 yards

Kaupungin Talvipuutarha (Winter Garden)

Near the Olympic Stadium, this vast collection of glasshouses is a tropical paradise perfect for a winter's day. Step inside to stroll beneath towering palms and Norfolk Island pines, and to revel in the passion flowers and camellias that bloom through the winter. Christmas and Easter bring indoor displays of flowers and in the summer the outdoor rose gardens are spectacular. ➌ Hammarskjöldintie 1 ❶ 09 3103 9985 🕐 09.00–15.00 Tues, 12.00–15.00 Wed–Fri, 12.00–16.00 Sat & Sun Ⓜ Tram 8

Linnanmäki Amusement Park

From the original 1951 wooden roller coaster to the latest in high-tech thrills, Linnanmäki is fun for all ages. With 43 rides in total, there are 11 specifically for children, 17 suitable for whole families, and 15 major rides which older visitors will enjoy including a fun house and a hall of mirrors. The park is run by a children's charity foundation and ticket money goes to a good cause. Live shows are performed daily on the outdoor stage and a free play area, Fairytale Valley, is always there for children. ➌ Tivolikuja 1 ❶ 09 773 991 Ⓦ www.linnanmaki.fi 🕐 May–early Sept (hours vary) Ⓜ Tram: 3B, 9, bus: 23. Admission charge for rides (entry to area is free)

Olympiastadion (Olympic Stadium)

Built in 1938 by functionalist architects Yrjö Lindegren and Toivo Jäntti, for the 1940 Olympics, the stadium was not used because World War II intervened and the Games were cancelled. It was not until the summer of 1952 that the Olympics finally came to the stadium, which is now a venue for athletic and music events. Outside is a statue of runner Paavo Nurmi, 'The Flying Finn', who won the gold medal, and carried the Olympic torch the last lap into the stadium for the 1952 Olympiad.

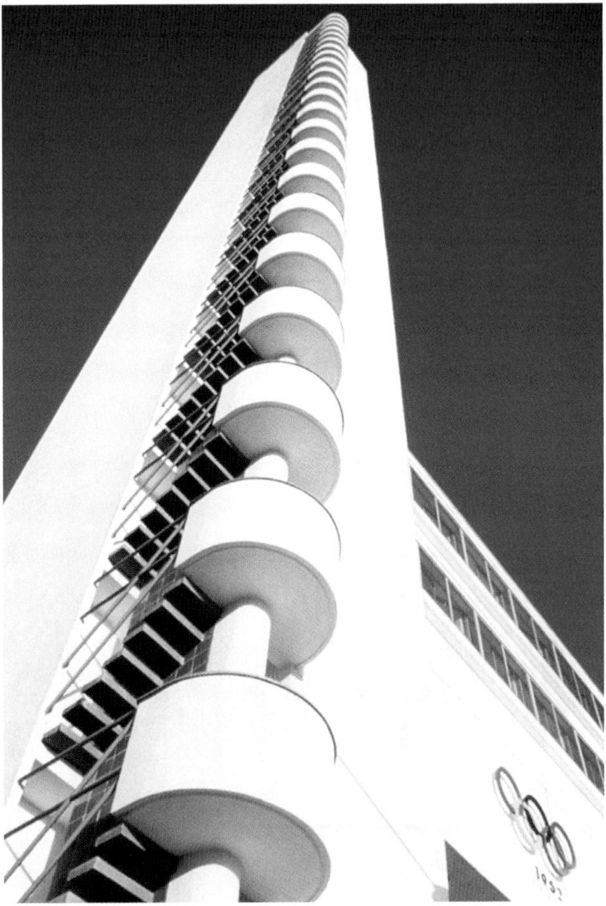

The Olympic Tower is the epitome of 1930s style

The stadium's 72 m (236 ft) tower gives a panoramic view of the city and over the Gulf of Finland, and also at the stadium is the Museum of Finnish Sports. To get there, take the first right from Mannerheimintie after Helsinginkatu or take tram 3T to Nordenskiöldinkatu and walk south on Pohjoinen stadiontie. ⓐ Paavo Nurmentie 1 ❶ Stadium: 09 4366 010; museum: 09 434 2250 Ⓦ Stadium: www.stadion.fi; museum: www.urheilumuseo.org ⓛ Stadium: 09.00–20.00 Mon–Fri, 09.00–18.00 Sat & Sun (closed during events); museum: 11.00–19.00 Mon–Fri, 12.00–16.00 Sat & Sun Ⓝ Tram: 3T, 4T, 7, 10. Admission charge

Sea Life Helsinki
The underwater world of the local Baltic waters, the Arctic and the tropical seas are explored in this series of underwater exhibits. A transparent tunnel takes visitors through these underwater worlds

◯ *Some like it, some don't, but you can't ignore the Sibelius Monument*

to see creatures from starfish to sharks. Environmental impact of human activity is a major theme, dealing with issues such as pollution and the unrestrained harvesting of fish. Aim to be there during feeding times – ask for details at the entrance. 🅰 Tivolitie 10 📞 09 565 8200 🌐 www.sealife.fi 🕐 10.00–17.00 Thur–Tues, 10.00–20.00 Wed, Oct–Apr; 10.00–19.00 Mon–Sat, 10.00–17.00 Sun, May & June and Aug & Sept; 10.00–21.00 July 🚋 Tram: 3B, 9. Admission charge

Sibelius-monumentti (Sibelius Monument)
The great Finnish composer once said that 'Nobody erects a monument to a critic' – and thus expressed a frustration of artists everywhere. He needn't have worried about his own legacy – not only a monument, but an entire Sibelius Park to accommodate it – although the critics had much to say about the monument. Designed by Eila Hiltunen, it was unveiled in 1967, and was immediately subjected to a barrage of criticism. Composed of a collection of large metal pipes that catch the wind, the monument creates its own music. Later, in response to the complaints that people didn't 'identify' with the composer through this monument, a more conventional statue of him was added. The park is a nice place to stroll or take a picnic. 🅰 Sibelius Park, Mechelininkatu 38 (Taka-Töölö) 🕐 Daylight hours 🚌 Bus: 18, 24

Temppeliaukion kirkko (Temppeliaukio Church or Church in the Rock)
Nowhere is the Finns' fascination with architectural experiments more evident than in the Church in the Rock, one of the city's most visited attractions. The notion of carving an entire church out of solid rock is not new, but such troglodyte chapels are rarely cut into a relatively small outcrop in the middle of a city. However, that's exactly what architects Timo and Tuomo Suomalainen did, covering the excavation with a roof of woven copper connected to concrete spokes.

The rounded copper roof offsets the deadening effect of the granite walls, creating extraordinary acoustics for concerts, which can range from Christmas chorales to klezmer groups. ❷ Lutherinkatu 3, off Fredrikinkatu ❶ 09 2340 5920 ❷ 10.00–20.00 Mon, Tues, Thur & Fri, 10.00–18.45 Wed, 10.00–18.00 Sat, 11.45–13.45, 15.30–18.00 Sun, mid-May–mid-Sept; 10.00–17.00 Mon, 10.00–12.45, 14.15–17.00 Tues, 10.00–18.00 Wed, 10.00–20.00 Thur & Fri, 10.00–18.00 Sat, 11.45–13.45, 15.30–18.00 Sun, mid-Sept–mid-May. Hours may vary due to services and concerts ❷ Bus: 18, 24; tram: 3T

CULTURE

Although the area west of Mannerheimintie is better known for its shopping and nightlife than for its cultural attractions, you'll find three art museums, a car museum and one highlighting Finland's relation to other world cultures.

At the far western edge, the Kaapelitehdas (Cable Factory) is a multi-faceted complex of small museums, with a theatre and restaurant.

⬇ *The city's most unusual church was hollowed out from granite*

KAAPELITEHDAS (CABLE FACTORY)

The renovated factory overlooking the western docks, a combination of sights under one roof, houses the following trio of small museums and two dance theatre groups, as well as a restaurant. ❸ Tallberginkatu 1 ① 09 4763 8300 ⓦ www.kaapelitehdas.fi ⓝ Bus/tram: 8, 15, 20, 21, 65A, 66A. Admission charge

Dance Theatre Hurjaruuth This theatre specialises in children's dance performances. ① 09 565 7250 ⓦ www.hurjaruuth.fi

Finnish Museum of Photography This museum explores the history and artistry of photography from 1840 to the present. ① 09 686 63621 ⓦ www.valokuvataiteenmuseo.fi ⓛ 11.00–18.00 Tues–Sun

Hotel and Restaurant Museum Take a look at Finnish food and drink traditions. ① 09 6859 3700 ⓦ www.hotellijaravintolamuseo.fi ⓛ 11.00–18.00 Tues–Sun

Theatre Museum This museum offers special exhibits on the history and art of the stage, but its primary focus is on interaction, so visitors can play with the exhibits and try their hand at various forms of theatre art. ① 0207 961 670 ⓦ www.teatterimuseo.fi ⓛ 11.00–18.00 Tues–Sun

Zodiak Centre for New Dance This centre is a repertory company that explores trends in dance though regular performances. ① 09 694 4948 ⓦ www.zodiak.fi

Helsingin automuseo (Helsinki Car Museum)

If model cars race your engines, don't miss Europe's largest collection of over 3,000 miniature autos. The real things are there, too, and the collection of vintage autos – everything from a 1931 taxi to the cars of Finnish presidents – is enlivened by wax figures of the famous Finns who owned them. ⓐ Munkkisaarenkatu 12 ⓣ 09 667 123 ⓦ www.automuseo.fi ⓛ 12.00–15.00 Thur–Sun ⓝ Tram: 1A; bus: 14B, 16. Admission charge

Helsingin kaupungin taidemuseo (Helsinki City Art Museum)

Special exhibitions of Finnish and international art are shown here, often part of an international circuit. ⓐ Tennispalatsi, Salomonkatu 15 (near the Kamppi shopping centre) ⓣ 09 310 87001 ⓦ www.taidemuseo.hel.fi ⓛ 11.00–20.30 Tues–Sun ⓝ Metro: Kamppi. Admission charge

Kulttuurien museo (Museum of Cultures)

The permanent 'Fetched from Afar' exhibition in this fascinating museum explores the Finno-Ugric peoples (see page 22), as well as telling the story of other cultures through the work of early Finnish explorers and anthropologists. Part of the museum focuses on Chinese artefacts brought to Finland by traders and seafarers in the early 19th century. ⓐ Salomonkatu 15 ⓣ 09 405 09806 ⓛ 11.00–20.00 Tues, 11.00–18.00 Wed–Sun ⓝ Metro: Kamppi. Admission charge

Sinebrychoffin taidemuseo (Sinebrychoff Art Museum)

Finland's finest collection of Old Masters and other European art from the 1300s to the 1800s is displayed in the furnished mansion of the museum's donors. The rooms, although used as galleries, have fine parquet floors and other interior features. Miniatures

and porcelain collections are especially impressive. ⓐ Bulevardi 40
ⓣ 09 1733 6460 ⓦ www.sinebrychoffintaidemuseo.fi ⓛ 10.00–18.00
Tues & Fri, 10.00–20.00 Wed & Thur, 11.00–17.00 Sat & Sun
ⓝ Tram: 6. Admission charge

Taidehalli (Kunsthalle)

Changing exhibitions of contemporary art highlight young artists as
well as those who have already established a reputation. Taidehallin
Klubi, the gallery's restaurant, is open for lunch and evening meals
Monday–Saturday and the bar is open Monday–Saturday until
02.00. ⓐ Nervanderinkatu 3 ⓣ 09 454 2060 ⓦ www.taidehalli.fi
ⓛ 11.00–18.00 Tues, Thur & Fri, 11.00–20.00 Wed, 11.00–17.00 Sat
& Sun ⓝ Bus: 24. Admission charge

RETAIL THERAPY

The lovely Fredrikinkatu and the streets adjoining it are known for
their fashion and interior-décor boutiques. Stroll Bulevardi to browse
or buy art and antiques. Forum is the biggest shopping complex in
the city centre, with more than 100 shops, facing onto Mannerheimintie
(number 20) and filling the entire area between it and Yrjönkatu.
Kamppi shopping centre has a variety of designer shops, restaurants
and cafés, and is conveniently located above the main bus station
(see page 51).

Aero Find a piece of vintage Alvar Aalto, or the work of other
Finnish designers in this shop that specialises in 1930–1970
Finnish design and furnishings. ⓐ Yrjönkatu 8 ⓣ 09 680 2185
ⓦ www.aerodesignfurniture.fi ⓛ 10.00–18.00 Mon–Fri, 11.00–15.00
Sat ⓝ Tram: 3B, 6, 9, 10

Antiq Bulevard It won't be cheap, but it will be good if you find it in this high-class antiquerie. Hours are eccentric, so call or just stop in if it's open. ⓐ Vuorimiehenkatu 10 ⓣ 040 552 1764 ⓝ Tram: 1A, 3B, bus: 16

Bisarri Here you'll find modern Finnish design alongside glassware, ceramics, textiles and gorgeous utility items. ⓐ Hietalahti Market Hall, Hietalahdentori ⓣ 09 611 252 ⓦ www.bisarri.fi ⓛ 10.00–17.00 Mon–Fri, 10.00–15.00 Sat ⓝ Tram: 6

Galerie 1900 Art nouveau's back with a 'V' and, of course, Helsinki's the place to find it. The shop offers lighting fixtures and decor items in Jugendstil and art deco style. ⓐ Annankatu 11 ⓣ 09 649 152 ⓛ Hours vary; call before visiting ⓝ Tram: 10

Helsinki 10 Trendy shop of vintage designer clothes, music and art books. ⓐ Eerikinkatu 3 ⓣ 050 559 6504 ⓦ www.helsinki10.com ⓛ 11.00–20.00 Mon–Fri, 11.00–18.00 Sat ⓝ Tram: 3B, 3T, 6, 9, 10

Hietalahti Flea Market Be prepared to bargain for everything from cut-price clothes to antiques. The latter may include the family treasures of someone settling an estate or just cleaning house, as well as regular dealers. ⓐ Hietalahdentori ⓛ 08.00–19.00 Mon–Fri, 08.00–16.00 Sat, 10.00–16.00 Sun, May–Sept; 09.00–17.00 Mon–Fri, 08.00–16.00 Sat, Oct–Apr ⓝ Tram: 6

Hietalahti Market Hall Architect Selim Lindqvist's historic building, across the square from the flea market, is filled with shops and stalls selling local handicrafts, plus cafés. ⓐ Hietalahdentori ⓛ 10.00–17.00 Mon–Fri, 10.00–15.00 Sat ⓝ Tram: 6

Ivana Helsinki Campus Visionary stylish clothes for an easy lifestyle, Ivana's clothes are rich in outdoor themes and designed to be lived in. ⓐ Uudenmaankatu 15 ☎ 09 622 4422 ⓦ www.ivanahelsinki.com ⏱ 11.00–19.00 Mon–Fri, 11.00–16.00 Sat ⓝ Tram: 3B, 6

Limbo Shop Limbo's easy styles flow with the season, from comfortable sundresses in cheery colours to sweats and t-shirts with a sense of humour. Hip clothes don't get more comfortable. ⓐ Annankatu 13 ☎ 09 644 060 ⓦ www.limbo.fi ⏱ 11.00–18.00 Mon–Fri, 11.00–16.00 Sat ⓝ Tram: 3B, 6, 9

Lux Shop This shop sells one-of-a-kind fashions by creative young designers, including the fashion pieces rich in printing, embroidery and applique by Rinne Niinikoski. ⓐ Uudenmaankatu 26 ☎ 09 678 538 ⓦ www.lux-shop.fi ⏱ 12.00–18.00 Mon–Sat ⓝ Tram: 3B, 6

Miun You like Finnish designer clothing, jewellery, accessories and ceramic statues? Come here now. ⓐ Uudenmaankatu 14 ☎ 050 303 0530 ⓦ www.miun.fi ⏱ 12.00–18.00 Mon–Fri, 11.00–16.00 Sat ⓝ Tram: 3B, 6, 9

Myymälä2 A plain-jane environment where young artists can show their work, Myymala2 has launched several talents, as well as creating a venue for gallery-goers. The boutique is a gold-mine of groovy gifts and funky finds. ⓐ Uudenmaankatu 23 ☎ No phone ⓦ www.myymala2.com ⏱ 12.00–18.00 Wed–Sat, 12.00–17.00 Sun ⓝ Tram: 3B, 6

Nemaki A swish boutique offering luxury clothes by Scandinavian designer Irja Leimu. ⓐ Tarkk'ampujankatu 20 ☎ 09 631 353 ⏱ 12.00–17.00 Tues–Fri, 12.00–14.00 Sat ⓝ Tram: 3B

Popparienkeli Whatever you need in new or used vinyl from the 1950s and 60s or CDs from the 80s onwards, you're likely to find it here. But ask, since not everything is displayed. Look for other music shops in this vicinity. ⓐ Fredrikinkatu 12 ❶ 09 661 638 Ⓦ www.popangel.fi Ⓛ 10.00–18.00 Mon–Fri, 10.00–16.00 Sat Ⓝ Tram: 3B

Punavuoren Peikko The coolest shop in Helsinki for kids' clothes and toys, many by Scandinavian designers. ⓐ Uudenmaankatu 15 ❶ 045 120 0823 Ⓦ www.punavuorenpeikko.fi Ⓛ 10.30–18.00 Mon–Fri, 10.30–16.00 Sat Ⓝ Tram: 3B, 6, 9, 10

Le Slip Shop for undergarments at uber-prices, all from the best designers. ⓐ Annankatu 6 ❶ 09 640 762 Ⓛ 11.00–18.00 Mon–Fri, 11.00–15.00 Sat Ⓝ Tram: 3B

Stupido Shop If it's on DVD, tape, CD or vinyl, and it's alternative, from humppa to the latest Aavikko, just ask the Stupido guys. ⓐ Iso Roobertinkatu 23 Ⓦ www.stupido.fi Ⓛ 09.00–20.00 Mon–Fri, 10.00–18.00 Sat Ⓝ Tram: 3B

TAKING A BREAK

The mega-malls Forum and Kamppi both have a number of cafés and small eating places. It's a good rule that wherever shoppers congregate, there will be places to stop for coffee and compare finds.

Belly ££ ❶ If you have a licence to enjoy a bag of nuts and a mocktail, this 1960s- and 1970s-style restaurant has its own James Bond bar. If you like soul and funk, you'll be in double-O heaven. ⓐ Uudenmaankatu 16–20 ❶ 09 644 981 Ⓦ www.belly.fi

🕐 10.30–16.00 Mon–Thur, 10.30–04.00 Fri, 18.00–04.00 Sat
🚋 Tram: 3B, 6

Café Bar no. 9 ££ ② Cool and trendy place to eat during the day.
Good for drinks in the evening as well. 📍 Uudenmaankatu 9
📞 09 621 4059 🌐 www.bar9.net 🕐 11.00–02.00 Mon–Fri,
12.00–02.00 Sat–Sun 🚋 Tram: 3B, 6, 9, 10

Café Ekberg ££ ③ Helsinki's oldest café, Ekberg isn't just a period
piece, it's a bit of romantic old Europe. Reminiscent of between-the-
wars Vienna, it's the kind of place you expect to see writers working
on their books. They serve a breakfast buffet, lunch, light meals and
tasty pastries or a glass of something in between. 📍 Bulevardi 9

🔽 *People enjoy drinks at an outdoor café on Aleksanterinkatu*

🕿 09 6811 8660 🌐 www.cafeekberg.fi 🕐 07.30–19.00 Mon–Fri, 08.30–17.00 Sat, 09.00–17.00 Sun 🚋 Tram: 3B, 6

Tin Tin Tango ££ ❹ Something for everyone in this combination bar, self-serve laudromat, art gallery and sauna in the Töölö neighbourhood. 📍 Töölöntorinkatu 7 🕿 09 2709 0972 🕐 07.00–00.00 Mon–Thur, 07.00–02.00 Fri, 09.00–02.00 Sat, 10.00–00.00 Sun 🚋 Tram: 3T, 8

AFTER DARK

Along with having some of the hottest clubs and entertainment venues in the city, the neighbourhoods away from the Esplanadi are also the 'low rent district' for bars and pubs. Iso Roobertinkatu is known for its restaurants, pubs and bars, which fill almost the entire street. While a number of places have age limits that cut out those below 20 or 24, most of the places around the Kamppi metro station do not, so traditionally, this is where the under-20s hang out.

RESTAURANTS

Rafla ££ ❺ Modern European cuisine with a touch of French and Scandinavian home cooking. Excellent espresso, good wines and nice atmosphere. 📍 Uudenmaankatu 9 🕿 09 6124 2244 🌐 www.ravintolarafla.fi 🕐 11.00–02.00 Mon–Fri, 13.00–02.00 Sat 🚋 Tram: 3B, 6, 9

Cosmos ££–£££ ❻ A Helsinki institution since 1924, serving delicious classic dishes from duck and chateaubriand to champagne sorbet and pancakes. 📍 Kalevankatu 3 🕿 09 647 255 🌐 www.ravintolacosmos.fi 🕐 11.30–01.00 Mon–Fri, 16.00–01.00 Sat 🚇 Metro: Kamppi

Demo ££–£££ ❼ High-class homemade food combined with personal and friendly service. Recently awarded a Michelin star. ⓐ Uudenmaankatu 9–11 ☎ 09 2289 0840 ⓦ www.restaurantdemo.fi ⏱ 16.00–23.00 Tues–Sat Ⓝ Tram: 3B, 6, 9, 10

Helmi ££–£££ ❽ The stylish décor sets the tone for equally well designed dishes. The inspiration is global and eclectic, and the vegetarian dishes are as well planned and original as the other choices – taro chips and mushroom mousse might accompany a tofu steak. Even the plain-sounding dish of chicken and vegetables is a winner. Minimum age is 24. ⓐ Eerikinkatu 14 ☎ 09 612 6410 ⓦ www.helmi.net ⏱ 17.00–00.00 Tues–Thur, 17.00–04.00 Fri & Sat Ⓝ Metro: Kamppi

Lappi ££–£££ ❾ Not just Finnish, but only those dishes originating in Lapland are the speciality of this cosy restaurant. Reindeer and other game meats are featured, along with salmon in several forms and boutique farm-made cheeses. The authentic atmosphere of natural wood furnishings and soft lighting is pleasant, too. ⓐ Annankatu 22 ☎ 09 645 550 ⓦ www.lappires.com ⏱ 12.00–00.00 Mon–Fri, 13.00–00.00 Sat, summer; 12.00–22.30 Mon–Fri, 13.00–22.30 Sat, winter Ⓝ Tram: 3B, 6

Lehtovaara ££–£££ ❿ The menu speaks for itself at this exceptional restaurant near the Sibelius Park: fillet of beef with deep-fried garlic potatoes, garlic butter and fried fresh mushroom slices, lightly smoked Arctic char with lobster ravioli or snowgrouse breast with a cake of root vegetables and potato. Vegetarians might be offered cheese polenta with ginger-braised vegetables. ⓐ Mechelininkatu 39 ☎ 09 440 833 ⓦ www.lehtovaararavintola.fi ⏱ 11.00–00.00 Mon–Fri, 16.00–00.00 Sat, 13.00–21.00 Sun Ⓝ Bus: 18, 24, 42

Ravintola Carelia & Winebar £££ ⑪ The wine list alone is staggering, with over 300 varieties, including 50 different champagnes, making it a good place to stop before or after the opera, just across the street. Menu choices are just as difficult. Begin maybe with cep soup with thyme foam, then go on to guinea fowl breast with truffle risotto and bacon. ⓐ Mannerheimintie 56 ⓣ 09 2709 0976 ⓛ 11.00–00.00 Mon–Fri, 16.00–00.00 Sat ⓝ Tram: 3T, 4, 7, 10

BARS & CLUBS

Armas A party pub in the centre of town. Dance on the tables, sing karaoke or just listen to the top Finnish hits. ⓐ Simonkatu 8 ⓣ No phone ⓦ www.armashelsinki.fi ⓛ 21.00–03.00 Wed, Fri & Sat ⓝ Metro: Kamppi

Cuba As well as the best mojitos in town, this place has DJs and wild late-night parties. ⓐ Erottajankatu 4 ⓣ 050 325 9522 ⓦ www.cubacafe.fi ⓛ 17.00–02.00 Tues–Thur, 17.00–04.00 Fri & Sat ⓝ Tram: 10

Dante's Highlight Back in 1878 this building was a church; now it's a raucous three-storey nightclub with several dance floors, a wide range of music and a young clientele – it's one of the few clubs that admit 18-year-olds. ⓐ Fredrikinkatu 42 ⓣ 010 766 3780 ⓦ www.danteshighlight.fi ⓛ 12.00–04.00 Mon–Fri, 16.00–04.00 Sat & Sun ⓝ Metro: Kamppi. Admission charge (free 22.00–23.00)

DTM No-one has disputed DTM's claim to be the biggest combo of gay café, bar, disco and nightclub in Scandinavia. Taking it from the top, the upstairs has a cruise ship-style dance floor with disco and traditional dance music on Friday and Saturday. The street level is a café, with internet access. Downstairs, the nightclub has live music, dance and shows, with a killer sound system and over-the-top lighting and video tech. Special nights offer top drag shows, bubbling foam parties and more. Minimum age 18 between 18.00 and 21.00; after 21.00 it's 24 (those younger will be ejected). ⓐ Iso Roobertinkatu 28 ⓣ 010 841 6969 ⓦ www.dtm.fi ⓛ 09.00–04.00 Mon–Sat, 12.00–04.00 Sun ⓝ Tram: 3B. Admission charge from 00.00 Sat

Lost and Found Gay, straight, whatever. Everyone is welcome and feels at home in this modern restaurant/club/bar/disco. Call it Lostari, to feel like a local. Best to go early, since queues form on the big party nights – Wednesday, Friday, Saturday – before midnight. Age 22 and over. ⓐ Annankatu 6 ⓣ 09 680 1010 ⓦ www.lostandfound.fi ⓛ 20.00–04.00 ⓝ Tram 3B

O'Malley's A Finnish take on an Irish pub, but a good stop for a pint if you're over 20. ⓐ Sokos Hotel, Yrjönkatu 26 ⓣ 09 4336 6330 ⓛ 16.00–01.00 Mon–Thur, 16.00–02.00 Fri & Sat, 18.00–00.00 Sun ⓝ Tram: 3T

Royal Onnela Big disco, table-dancing and a section for metal, this place is especially popular because the €5 membership card buys you beers for €1 from 23.00 to 01.00 most nights. ⓐ Fredrikinkatu 48 ⓣ 020 775 9460 ⓦ www.ravintolaonnela.fi ⓛ 22.00–04.00 Wed–Sat, 23.00–04.00 Sun ⓝ Metro: Kamppi

Storyville The city's premier jazz club, Storyville offers live jazz in an environment that favours listening to the New Orleans-style music and enjoying a drink. The pub upstairs provides a place to wait for the crowd to thin on weekends. ⓐ Museokatu 8 ⓣ 09 408 007

ⓦ www.storyville.fi ⓛ 19.00–03.00 Tues, 19.00–04.00 Wed–Sat
ⓝ Tram: 4, 7, 10. Admission charge

Tavastia You can witness the country's major bands in action
at Finland's leading rock venue. ⓐ Urho Kekkosen katu 4–6
ⓘ 09 774 67423 ⓦ www.tavastiaklubi.fi ⓛ 21.00–02.00
Sun–Thur, 21.00–03.00 Fri & Sat ⓝ Metro: Kamppi

The Tiger The classiest club in town is on two floors on top of the
Kamppi shopping centre. Large dance floors and top quality sound
systems – what more could you want? ⓐ Urho Kekkosen katu 1
ⓘ 020 775 9350 ⓦ www.thetiger.fi ⓛ 22.00–04.00 Wed–Sat
ⓝ Metro: Kamppi

ENTERTAINMENT

Tennispalatsi The indoor tennis stadium was built in 1938 for the
Olympics that never happened, but the Finns have put it to good
use as a sports area and entertainment venue. Among other things,
it contains the Helsinki City Art Museum and Museum of Cultures
(see page 95), a **14-screen cinema** (ⓘ 0600 007 007 ⓦ www.finnkino.fi
ⓛ Box office from 10.00) and numerous cafés and restaurants. Nearby
is the Kamppi shopping centre (see page 96) and bus station. It's a great
place to visit on a rainy day or if you have kids in tow, as there's plenty
to keep you occupied all day. ⓐ Salomonkatu 15 ⓝ Metro: Kamppi

The islands & outskirts

Helsinki sits in the midst of an archipelago and some of its most outstanding attractions are on the islands. Chief among them is the World Heritage Site of Suomenlinna Fortress, which consists of a small cluster of islands interconnected by bridges and sandbars. On Suomenlinna you'll find enough museums, craft studios and restaurants to keep you occupied all day. Animal lovers will enjoy Korkeasaari Zoo, where rare animals have plenty of room to roam. Those hankering after some time on the beach can head to Pihlajasaari or Uunisaari islands. As well as dedicated excursion boats which tour the archipelago, there are frequent ferries to Suomenlinna throughout the year and to the other main islands in the summer months. Ferry trips provide an inexpensive way of getting afloat and are included in the Helsinki Card (see page 58).

SIGHTS & ATTRACTIONS

Boat trips

You can enjoy the views of elegant Helsinki and get a cheap mini-cruise by taking the ferry between Kauppatori (Market Square) and Suomenlinna Fortress. Boats for Suomenlinna leave less frequently from Katajanokka, east of Market Square. For timetables see Ⓦ www.hkl.fi or ask at the tourist office.

In the summer months ferries also travel from Market Square to Korkeasaari, where the zoo is located, and continue on to Hakaniemenranta quay in the Kallio neighbourhood behind the railway station, where there is another daily market. Another ferry leaves from the southern tip of the city (in the Eira neighbourhood), bound for Pihlajasaari, a beach-ringed island west of Suomenlinna.

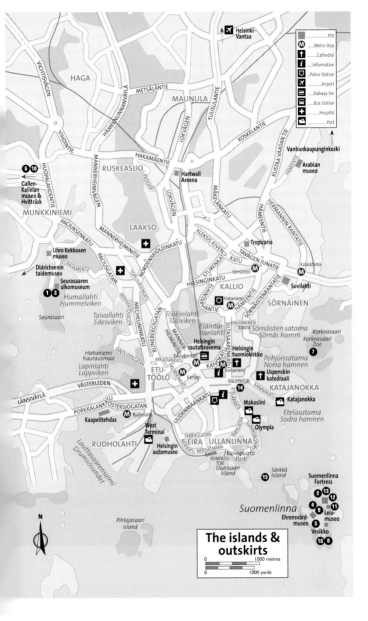

The islands & outskirts

Legend

- ◼ ...... POI
- Ⓜ ...... Metro Stop
- ✝ ...... Cathedral
- ⓘ ...... Information
- 🛇 ...... Police Station
- ✈ ...... Airport
- 🚉 ...... Railway Stn
- 🚌 ...... Bus Station
- ✚ ...... Hospital
- ⚓ ...... Port

✈ Helsinki-Vantaa

HAGA

MAUNULA

VICHTISVÄGEN

HÄMEENLINNANVÄYLÄ
METSÄLÄNTIE

VIHDINTIE

TUUSULANTIE

LOKVÄGEN

KOSKELANTIE

HAKAMÄENTIE

Vanhankaupunginkoski

❽ ❿
Gallen-Kallelan museo & Hvitträsk

HUOPALAHDENTIE

RUSKEASUO

Hartwall Areena

Arabian museo

HÄMEENTIE

MUNKKINIEMI

PACIUKSENKATU

MANNERHEIMVÄGEN

LAAKSO

NORDENSKIÖLDINKATU

ALEKSIS KIVENS KATU

MÄKELÄNKATU

HERMANNIN RANTATIE

KUSTAA VAASAN TIE

Uhro Kekkosen museo

PACIUSGATAN

TOPELIUSKATU

HELSINGINKATU

Tropicario

TAVÄGEN JUNATIE

Kalasatama

Didrichsenin taidemuseo

SEURASAARENTIE

MANNERHEIMINTIE

STURENKATU

Sörnäinen Ⓜ

Suvilahti

❶ ❸

Seurasaaren ulkomuseo

Humallahti
Hummelviken

KALLIO

Hakaniemi Ⓜ

SÖRNÄINEN

Seurasaari

Taivallahti
Edesviken

RUNEBERGSGATAN

MECHELININKATU

HUVUDSTA

Töölönlahti
Tölöviken

Eläintarhanlahti

Hakaniemenranta

SÖRNÄISTENRANTATIE

Sörnäisten satama
Sörnäs hamn

Korkeasaari
Korkeasaari Zoo ❼

Hietaniemi
hautausmaa

Lapinlahti
Lappviken

SANDUDDSGATAN

MANNER-
HEIMINTIE

Helsingin
rautatieasema

SIltasaarenkatu

KAISANIEMENRANTA

Helsingin
tuomiokirkko

Pohjoissatama
Norra hamnen

ETU-
TÖÖLÖ

ARKADIANKATU

Ⓜ Rautatientori

Kampti

Ⓜ Kampti

Kaisaniemi

Uspenskin
katedraali

VÄSTERLEDEN

KAUPPATORI

KATAJANOKKA

LÄNSIVÄYLÄ

PORKKALANKATU

ÖSTERSJÖGATAN

⚓ Ruoholahti

Kaapelitehdas

❹ ❶

Makasiini

Katajanokka

Eteläsatama
Södra hamnen

West
Terminal

UUDENMAANKATU

Olympia

Helsingin
automuseo

FABRIKSGATAN

EIRA

ULLANLINNA

RUOHOLAHTI

MERISATAMAN-
RANTA

KAIVOPUISTO
TORI

Kaivopuisto
Park

KOMPASSI

Lauttasaarensalmi
Drumsundet

Uunisaari
Island

Särkkä
Island

❶❺

Suomenlinna Fortress

❷ ❾ ❶❸ ❶❷

Suomenlinna

Ehrensvärd-
museo

Lelo-
museo

Pihlajasaari
Island

❶ ❺

Vesikko

❶❻ ❽

N

The islands & outskirts

| 0 | | 1000 metres |
| 0 | | 1000 yards |

As boat timetables vary according to season and weather, it's best to consult the tourist office on arrival.

A number of traditional cruise boats ply the waters around Helsinki between May and September. **Sun Lines** (☎ 020 741 8210 ⓦ www.ihalines.fi) explores the tree-lined Degero Canal, Korkeasaari Zoo, the Finnish icebreakers and the cruise ship harbours, along with circling Suomenlinna sea fortress, in comfortable cruisers that offer a coffee and drinks bar. **IHA Lines** (☎ 09 6874 5050 ⓦ www.ihalines.fi) offer à la carte dining on their boats as they cruise through the archipelago on trips that last from 90 minutes to three hours. Three different routes, each beginning at Market Square, cover the eastern islands or the fortress and surrounding islands. Booking is essential for dining cruises. Along with archipelago cruises, **Royal Line** (ⓦ www.royalline.fi) offers daily trips to the medieval town of Porvoo in July and August (see page 124).

Korkeasaaren Eläintarha (Korkeasaari Zoo)

More than just a place for visitors to view exotic wildlife, Helsinki's zoo is a well-respected leader in the preservation and breeding of endangered species. Their snow leopard successes are legendary in zoo annals, and they continue to have rare species of the big cats. Currently these include, in addition to the snow leopards, Amur tiger, Siberian tiger, of which there are only a few hundred remaining, and the exceedingly rare Asian lion from India. Rare Arctic species include the polar fox and musk ox, whose protection from icy winters includes hair a metre (3 ft) long. Environments represented include tropical rainforests to arctic tundra, and the collections include 200 species of animals, with 1,000 species of plants to make them feel at home. Founded in 1889, it is one of the oldest zoos in the world. ⓐ Korkeasaari

◆ *Escape from the city to the tranquility of the forested islands*

🛈 0600 95 911 (24 hr info) or 09 310 1615 (switchboard)
Ⓦ www.korkeasaari.fi 🕑 10.00–20.00 May–Aug, 10.00–18.00 Sept, 10.00–16.00 Oct–Mar, 10.00–18.00 Apr 🚌 Bus: 11; ferry from Market Square or Hakaniemi Market May–Sept. Admission charge

Pihlajasaari Island

To get away from it all and luxuriate in the sun on an island in the Gulf of Finland, take the boat to the rocks and beaches of Pihlajasaari. Rent a private changing cabin or bare it all on the nudist beach. (You'll need clothes for the café, and for the boat ride!) 🛈 09 534 806 Ⓦ www.jt-line.fi 🕑 May–Sept 🚌 Boats depart Merisatamanranta

Suomenlinna Fortress

One of the world's largest sea fortresses, the 18th-century fort on Suomenlinna has a fascinating past and an interesting present. A 15-minute ferry ride from Market Square brings you to the group of connected islands, where there is enough to occupy an entire day – and in the summer, an evening, too. It was built in 1747 by the Swedes, who owned Finland then, to scare off the Russians, who eventually captured both it and Finland, turning the island's guns figuratively to the west. The impressive fortifications became a UNESCO World Heritage Site in 1991.

In the visitor centre a wide-screen show, 'The Suomenlinna Experience', explores the fortress's long history, in English. Sign up here for guided walks that help bring all the sites into a whole picture. In the same building is the museum, which paints a picture of how officers and soldiers lived during the Swedish and Russian rules. The fortress was also used by the Finns after independence as a prison for Communist detainees, a military garrison, a submarine base and the Valmet shipyard, which made ships as reparations for the Soviet Union after World War II.

Walking and cycling paths (you must bring cycles from the mainland as none are hired out here) lead along the cliffs and to small beaches. Be careful on the cliff paths, since these are not fenced, and when on the beaches with children, because of dangerous sudden ship wakes and currents. Various buildings house studios and shops of glassblowers, potters and other craftsmen. ❶ 09 684 1850 ⓦ www.suomenlinnatours.fi ❷ 10.00–16.00 ❷ Ferry from Kauppatori (daily) or Katajanokka (Mon–Fri); visit ⓦ www.hkl.fi for timetables

Uunisaari Island

Just off the southern tip of the city and reached by boat from Kompassitori near Kaivopuisto Park (mid-April–mid-Nov) or via a pontoon bridge (mid-Nov–mid-Apr), Uunisaari offers sand beaches with lifeguards, a café, a restaurant and a sauna. The well-protected beach is safe for children. ❶ 09 636 870 ⓦ www.uunisaari.com

CULTURE

Arabian museo (Arabia Museum)

The Arabia company began in 1874, and moved into the design of modern tableware in the 1930s. But it was not until the 1960s that it became a worldwide name in smart dinnerware and porcelain design. Follow the history of this well-known company, along with the development of Finnish and modern design in home furnishings in the museum, where 1,600 examples of utility and decorative porcelain from the past 125 years are shown. You'll also find the company's factory outlet shop here, with excellent bargains on imperfect and overstocked items. ❸ Hämeentie 135 ❶ 0204 3910

Ⓦ www.arabiamuseum.fi 🕐 12.00–18.00 Tues–Fri, 10.00–16.00
Sat & Sun Ⓝ Tram: 6, 8

Didrichsenin taidemuseo (Didrichsen Art Museum)

A couple's private collection is now a museum rich in 20th-century
art, along with specialised collections of Asian antiquities of the Shang
and Ming dynasties and pre-Columbian art of the Olmec, Jalisco and
Mayan cultures. Primary here is the Finnish art from the 20th century,
including works by Edelfelt and his contemporaries. Non-Finnish modern
art includes works by Picasso, Kandinsky and Miro. Ⓐ Kuusilahdenkuja 1,
Kuusisaari Ⓣ 09 477 8330 Ⓦ www.didrichsenmuseum.fi 🕐 11.00–18.00
Tues–Sun Ⓝ Bus: 194, 195 from Elielinaukio, bay 36 (near the post
office), 503, 506. Admission charge

Gallen-Kallelan museo (Gallen-Kallela Museum)

The most important Finnish artist of the early 1900s, Gallen-Kallela
had a rich and varied career in painting, drawing, graphics, sculpture,
posters, photographs and applied art, all of which are represented in
this museum. It also tells about the artist's colourful life and times,
as well as his friends. Gallen-Kallela designed this Jugendstil home
and studio, built 1911–1913. The wooden Tarvaspää villa, built in the
1850s, houses a café. Ⓐ Gallen-Kallelantie 27, Espoo Ⓣ 09 849 2340
Ⓦ www.gallen-kallela.fi 🕐 10.00–18.00 mid-May–Aug; 11.00–16.00
Tues–Sat, 11.00–17.00 Sun, Sept–mid-May Ⓝ Tram: 4 to Munkkiniemi,
alight at Laajalahdenaukio, then walk through Munkinpuisto Park;
shuttle bus from Munkkiniemen puistotie Mon–Fri only.
Admission charge

Hvitträsk

If the artistic buzz of the Arts & Crafts and art nouveau period fires

MUSEUMS ON SUOMENLINNA

There are three interesting museums on the cluster of islands that make up Suomenlinna, although note that they are only open during summer. The **Ehrensvärd-museo** (Ehrensvärd Museum ☎ 09 684 1850 🕐 10.00–17.00 mid-May–Aug; 11.00–16.00 Sept), in the former home of the fort's designer and commander Augustin Ehrensvärd, depicts the earliest Swedish period with models, arms, furniture and paintings. The **Lelumuseo** (Doll and Toy Museum ☎ 040 500 6607 🌐 www.lelumuseo.fi 🕐 11.00–17.00 summer; open some weekends in winter) displays dolls, doll houses, teddy bears and other toys from the 1830s to the present. The old Russian villa in which the collection is located is well worth seeing in its own right. Lastly, you can also visit the 250–ton submarine **Vesikko** (☎ 0299 530 260 🕐 11.00–18.00 mid-May–Aug), which was originally commissioned by the German Navy but actually used by the Finnish Navy from 1936 until the end of World War II. ⓐ Suomenlinna 🌐 www.suomenlinna.fi

your imagination, it's worth the 30 km (18 mile) bus ride to visit the local shrine to this style, built as home and studio to some of its most illustrious lights. Designed by architects Herman Gesellius, Armas Lindgren and Eliel Saarinen, the log-and-stone home is the epitome of the National Romantic style. The architects all lived and worked there at some point, and it was here that the plans were drawn for the Helsinki Railway Station and others of the firm's most famous works. This was the boyhood home of Eliel's son, Eero Saarinen, known for designing American buildings and monuments such as the Gateway Arch in St Louis, Missouri. ⓐ Hvitträskintie 166, Luoma ① 09 4050 9630 Ⓦ www.nba.fi ⑤ 11.00–17.00 May–Sept; 11.00–17.00 Wed–Sun, Oct–Apr Ⓝ Bus: 165 from Kamppi bus terminal (bay 55) to Hvitträsk; train: L or U to Luoma. Admission charge

Seurasaaren Ulkomuseo (Seurasaari Open-air Museum)

Historic buildings from all over Finland have been moved to this outdoor museum, beautifully insulated from modern-day Helsinki on its own island. The village of 87 buildings centres around the farmstead, a working farm where livestock and crops are raised using old methods. Grander by far is the 18th-century Kahiluoto manor house, with its well-preserved interior, and the parsonage from Iisalmi. The oldest building preserved here is the wooden Karuna church from the 1600s. A regular series of workshops and programmes highlight folk life and traditional skills for visitors.
ⓐ Seurasaari ① 09 4050 9660 ⑤ 11.00–17.00 June–Aug; 09.00–15.00 Mon–Fri, 11.00–17.00 Sat & Sun, 2nd half May & early Sept Ⓝ Bus: 24. Admission charge

Summer Theatre

During summer, you have the chance to see traditional Finnish perfomances on Suomenlinna and Seurasaari islands. Productions are in Finnish but, apart from the occasional play, language is not a barrier to enjoyment since the programme is generally based on movement, action, dance and music. To buy tickets in advance, contact Lippupalvelu (see page 22) or visit the Stockmann or Sokos department stores (see page 79).

Urho Kekkosen museo (Kekkonen Museum)

The home of Finland's most famous president, Urho Kekkonen,

is a fine villa set in a park estate adjacent to the island of Seurasaari. Tamminiemi Villa was his official residence during his presidency, from 1956 to 1981. The villa is furnished with outstanding examples of Finnish design and art, as well as gifts of state. In the summer, the tour includes the sauna, which was the scene of a number of high-level meetings between Soviet and Western diplomats during the Cold War. ⓐ Seurasaarentie 15 ⓣ 09 4050 9650 ⓦ www.nba.fi ⓛ 11.00–17.00 mid-May–mid-Aug; 11.00–17.00 Wed–Sun, mid-Aug–mid-May ⓝ Bus: 24. Admission charge ⓘ The museum is undergoing renovations until 2011

RETAIL THERAPY

Outside the busy and trendy shopping streets of downtown Helsinki, the islands and outer suburbs nonetheless offer some quality shopping. The fortress of Suomenlinna houses a number of excellent artisan studios, and museum shops offer unique speciality gifts. And Arabia's factory outlet is a mecca for bargain hunters with a taste for fine dinnerware.

Arabia Factory Shop One of Scandinavia's best-known brands of porcelain and dinnerware, Arabia spans all ages and tastes with its classic lines and functional style. The outlet offers discontinued styles and seconds at deep discounts. Along with the Arabia label are goods in Iittala and other company brands. See page 111 for address and contact details. ⓛ 10.00–20.00 Mon–Fri, 10.00–16.00 Sat & Sun

Arts and Crafts Summer Shop Selected traditional and modern crafts in all media. ⓐ Suomenlinna B 34 ⓣ 050 408 2902 ⓛ 10.00–17.00 mid-May–Sept

Bastion Hårleman, Susisaari Artisans' studios, some of which are open to the public in the summer. You can call ahead to check, but it's easiest just to wander down on a sunny day and browse.
ⓐ Building B 31, Suomenlinna ⓣ 040 533 7903

Hvitträsk Museum Shop A source of the beautiful Kalevala and Kaunis *koru* jewellery, based on designs from Finnish folklore, this outstanding museum gift-shop also carries art and architecture

🔻 *All sorts of souvenirs are sold at Helsinki's excellent markets*

books and prints, and crafts made by the Friends of Finnish Handicrafts. The work of local artists includes glass art, jewellery, ceramics, sculpture, knitted woollens and linen tablecloths. **ⓐ** Hvittäskintie 166, Luoma **ⓣ** 09 4050 9630 **ⓦ** www.nba.fi **ⓛ** 11.00–17.00 May–Sept; 11.00–17.00 Wed–Sun, Oct–Apr **ⓝ** Trains: L and U to Luoma

Hytti ry This studio is a place where one can worship at the altar of the glass-blower's art. Phone to check opening times. **ⓐ** Building B 48, Suomenlinna **ⓣ** 09 668 727

Jetty Barracks Gallery Operated by the Helsinki Artists' Association, the gallery shows exhibitions of juried contemporary art in the rooms of the Jetty Barracks. **ⓐ** Iso Mustasaari, next to the Main Quay, Suomenlinna **ⓣ** 09 673 140 **ⓦ** www.helsingintaiteilijaseura.fi **ⓛ** 12.30–18.00 Tues–Thur, 11.30–16.00 Fri–Sun

Pot Viapori Ceramics Studio ⓐ Suomenlinna B 45 **ⓣ** 09 668 151 **ⓛ** 12.00–17.00 mid-July–late Aug

Safari Shop Korkeasaari Zoo's own brand of animal-themed and environmentally friendly products, as well as Fair Trade products and crafts from cooperatives in developing countries, are sold in the zoo's shop. **ⓐ** Korkeasaari **ⓣ** 09 696 2370 **ⓛ** 10.00–20.00 May–Aug, 10.00–18.00 Apr & Sept, 10.00–16.00 Oct–Mar

Seurasaari Museum Shop Traditional Finnish handicrafts, authentic sauna products, books and other historical items are available in the museum store. **ⓐ** Seurasaari **ⓣ** 09 4050 9662 **ⓛ** 11.00–17.00 June–Aug; 09.00–15.00 Mon–Fri, 11.00–17.00 Sat & Sun, late May & early Sept

TAKING A BREAK

Nearly every museum has its own café, usually open at least the same hours as the museum itself. Suomenlinna is well supplied with eating places, several of which are listed under After Dark on page 120, since they are also open for evening meals. For travel directions, see under the corresponding museum or attraction.

Café Antin Kaffeliiteri £ ❶ In a little shed building next to Antti farmstead, the café bakes traditional Finnish pastries and otherwise hard-to-find old-fashioned regional treats, including Karelian rice pastries and pancakes from the Aland Islands. The cinnamon rolls are addictive. ⓐ Seurasaari ❶ 09 4050 9660 ● 11.00–17.00 June–Aug; 09.00–15.00 Mon–Fri, 11.00–17.00 Sat & Sun, late May and early Sept

Café Vanille £ ❷ Opposite the church in the Russian merchants' quarter, cosy modern Café Vanille serves soups and sandwiches, along with freshly baked pastries, cappuccino, tea, hot cocoa and beer. ⓐ Building C 18, Suomenlinna ❶ 040 556 1169 ⓦ www.cafevanille.fi ● 11.00–18.00 June & mid Aug-Sept; 11.00–19.00 July–mid-Aug; open weekends only in winter

Seurasaari Island £ ❸ Several historic kiosks serve food and offer tables for those with picnics. The kiosk by the bridge (● 11.00–16.00 June–Aug) used to be in central Helsinki, and the kiosk in the Festival Grounds (● 11.00–16.00 Sat & Sun) has a grill available where you can barbecue your own food. ❶ 09 484 511

Café Bar Valimo ££ ❹ The grass-roofed ammunition foundry that houses this summer café is located on the docks near an old wooden sailing vessel and the guest harbour. Valimo serves soups, pasta dishes, snacks, sandwiches and soft drinks, as well as having a full alcohol licence. **a** Building B 13, Suomenlinna **t** 09 692 6450 **w** www.valimo.org **L** 11.00–22.30 Mon–Thur, 11.00–22.30 Fri & Sat, 11.00–18.30 Sun, May–mid-June; 10.30–22.30 Mon–Sat, 10.30–20.30 Sun, mid-June–mid-Aug. Closes earlier late Aug

Café Piper ££ 5 In a charming old wooden villa set in a park, with a terrace overlooking the sea, Café Piper serves soup, savoury snacks, pastries and drinks including beer. **a** Building B 56, Suomenlinna **t** 09 684 1850 **L** 10.00–17.00 May; 10.00–19.00, June–mid-Aug; 10.00–17.00, mid-Aug–mid-Sept

Hvitträsk ££ 6 Located in the estate's Little Villa, the Café Hvitträsk offers sandwiches and pastries, coffee, tea and alcoholic drinks in a charming atmosphere. On the second floor of the villa, the upmarket restaurant has a terrace for summer dining. An à la carte menu is offered in the evening. **a** Hvitträskintie 166, Luoma **t** 09 297 6033 **L** Café: 10.30–17.30; restaurant: 11.30–19.00 Wed–Sun

Korkeasaari Zoo ££ 7 A variety of kiosks and cafés serve snacks and lunches in the summer, including Café Karhu by the Bear Castle and Café Safari near the Mustikkamaa entrance. For a hot meal, visit Pukki Restaurant. All eateries are open during Zoo opening times (see page 109). **t** Pukki Restaurant: 09 6962 3729

Pizzeria Nikolai ££ 8 Inside the stone casemates of Suomenlinna Fortress at King's Gate, Nikolai serves good pizza. In the summer, you can enjoy it on the terrace with a sea view. It's a good spot for

a break while exploring Suomenlinna's many attractions.
ⓐ Building A 10, Suomenlinna ⓣ 09 668 552 ⓛ 12.00–20.00
Mon–Sat, 12.00–18.00 Sun, May–Sept

Restaurant Café Chapman ££ ❾ Near the Visitor Centre, the year-
round café with a courtyard terrace is a lunch spot, and summer
evenings an à la carte restaurant. ⓐ Building B 1, Suomenlinna
ⓣ 010 841 9195 ⓛ 11.00–21.00 Mon–Fri, 12.00–21.00 Sat, 12.00–18.00
Sun, late May–mid-Sept; 10.30–15.00 Mon–Fri, mid Sept–early May

Tarvaspää ££ ❿ The villa was Gallen-Kallela's summer house
until 1913, when the studio was completed. The caféteria is now
there, serving traditional freshly baked Finnish pastries, including
cinnamon buns, called *korvapuusti*. ⓐ Gallen-Kallelantie 27, Espoo
ⓣ 09 849 2340 ⓦ www.gallen-kallela.fi ⓛ 10.00–18.00 Mon,
10.00–20.00 Tues–Thur, 10.00–18.00 Fri–Sun, mid-May–Aug;
11.00–16.00 Tues–Sat, 11.00–17.00 Sun, Sept-mid May

Toy Museum Café ££ ⓫ Tucked into the wooden Russian villa with
the Toy Museum, this cosy tearoom and terrace serves Russian-style
tea, real lemonade and freshly baked pastries, including wonderful
apple pie. ⓐ Building C 66, Suomenlinna ⓣ 040 500 6607 ⓛ 11.00–16.00
Sat & Sun, Apr; 11.00–16.00 late May; 11.00–17.00 June; 11.00–18.00
July; 11.00–17.00 Aug; 11.00–16.00 Sat & Sun, Sept

AFTER DARK

Apart from the islands of Suomenlinna, most of the 'museum
islands' are daytime destinations. One or two restaurants might
offer evening meals, but the city's nightlife is centred in its mainland

neighbourhoods. That said, if you plan to be at one of the outlying museums, such as Hvitträsk, in the late afternoon, their restaurants are well worth considering for their charm and their unhurried ambience.

RESTAURANTS

Suomenlinna Petty Officers' Club £–££ ⑫ Not fancy, but a favourite place for locals to meet, the club is in one of the old wooden buildings near the ferry landing. The terrace overlooks the city, across the water. ➌ Building C 8, Suomenlinna ① 09 668 273 ① 16.00–22.45 Mon–Thur, 16.00–23.45 Fri, 12.00–23.45 Sat, 12.00–19.45 Sun ① Closed mid–end Dec

Suomenlinna Panimo Brewery Restaurant ££ ⑬ The brewery, brewpub and restaurant are inside the high-vaulted casements of the Jetty Barracks, built during the Russian control of the fort. Sample the brewery's own Höpken Pils, Coyet Ale and the dark Helsinki Portteri. Booking is wise in the summer. ➌ Building C 1, Suomenlinna ① 09 228 5030 ① 15.00–22.00 Tues–Fri, 12.00–22.00 Sat, 12.00–18.00 Sun (subject to change)

Helsinki by Sea Dinner Cruise ££–£££ ⑭ Enjoy a changing land and seascape over dinner on board a sightseeing boat with a full kitchen. The à la carte menu offers starters such as forest mushroom cream soup or smoked salmon, and main courses including grilled breast of chicken in a gorgonzola sauce. Book in advance for these popular evening excursions. **IHA Lines** ① 09 6874 5050 ⓦ www.ihalines.fi ① 19.00 Tues–Sat, May–Sept

Restaurant Särkänlinna £££ ⑮ On the island of Särkkä between Suomenlinna and the southern tip of the city, the summer restaurant in a stone fortress offers stunning sea views and a setting rich in history. If you think the floor of the long dining room tilts a bit, you're right; it was designed to make it easier to get cannonballs to the cannons at the far end. ⓐ Särkkä ⓣ 09 1345 6756 ⓦ www.palacekamp.fi ⓛ 17.30–00.00 Mon–Sat, May–Sept ⓝ Reached by ferry from the Ullanlinna quay on the mainland at the southern end of the city

Walhalla Restaurant £££ ⓰ King's Gate is at the far end of the small island of Kustaanmiekka, part of the Suomenlinna island cluster, and Walhalla is set in the stone-arched interior of the fortress there. It's worth the ferry ride – an enjoyable evening trip – to savour such starters as mousse of smoked Arctic char with whitebait roe, or main courses such as fillet of reindeer with morel sauce. You can end a meal with equally traditional local ingredients: try cloudberry charlotte with cloudberry melba. The views from the terrace bar are just as outstanding. Be sure to book ahead. ⓐ Building A 10, Suomenlinna ⓣ 09 668 552 ⓦ www.restaurantwalhalla.com ⓛ 18.00–00.00 Mon–Sat

▶ *The forbidding keep of Finland's largest castle is one of the sights of Turku*

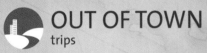
OUT OF TOWN
trips

Porvoo

Porvoo lies 50 km (30 miles) northeast of Helsinki and is Finland's second-oldest town, dating from the 1500s. Today the town is known for its small shops specialising in crafts and antiques and is a perfect day-trip destination. The best way to reach Porvoo is by boat, as you can see the beautiful archipelago on the way there. **J L Runeberg** (☎ 019 524 3331 🌐 www.msjlruneberg.fi) and **Royal Line** (☎ 020 711 8333 🌐 www.royalline.fi) both offer trips to Porvoo during the summer months. Departing from Market Square in the morning, the cruise travels through the archipelago while guests enjoy lunch on board. Upon reaching the colourful old town, there are about two hours to explore its cathedral, wooden buildings and narrow lanes lined with shops and cafés, before the return voyage to Helsinki. **Porvoo Tourist Office** ⓐ Rihkamakatu 4 ☎ 019 520 2316 🌐 www.porvoo.fi 🕐 09.00–18.00 Mon–Fri, 10.00–16.00 Sat & Sun, June–Aug; 09.00–16.30 Mon–Fri, 10.00–14.00 Sat, Sept–May

GETTING THERE

Porvoo is only about a thirty-minute drive from Helsinki. If you don't want to take a boat cruise (see above), you can either drive there on Highway E18 or take a bus. Buses to Porvoo leave every 20–30 minutes from bays 1–4 of Kamppi bus station and one-way tickets cost around €12. For timetables, consult 🌐 www.matkahuolto.fi.

SIGHTS & ATTRACTIONS

Porvoo's picturesque riverfront is lined with little red wooden buildings that were once storehouses for the city's mercantile

◒ *Porvoo's many boutiques make it a popular day-trip destination*

Lappi
Eura
Köyliönjärvi
Säkylä
Vampula
Pyhäjärvi
Alastaro
Ylane
Oripää
Loimaa
Jokioinen
Forss
Mynäjoki
Poytyä
Mellila
Aurajoki
Karinainen
Mynämäki
Nousiainen
Aura
Koski
Somerc
Masku
Turku
Marttila
Raisio
Kuusjocki
Kiikala
Moomimaailma
Lieto
Paimio
Turku
Kuralan
kylämäki
E18
Pertteli
Salo
Sauvo
Muurla
Suomusjarvi
Pargas
Lohjanjä
Paimionselka
Perniö
Kisko
Kimito
Pohja
Gullkrona
fjärd
Dragsfjärd
Särkisalo
Tenala
Ka
Finland
Ekanas
Hanko

Kylmäkoski
Tampe
Pirkka
Urjala
Humppila

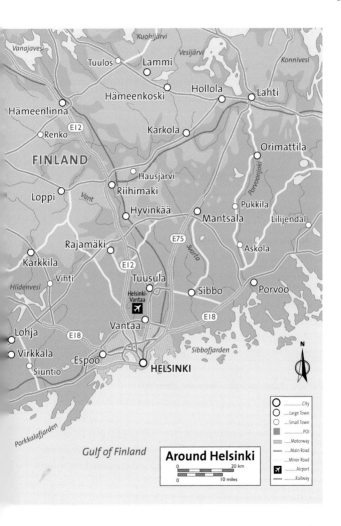

trade. The land rises from these to the old town, a charming tangle of old streets lined with ochre-coloured wooden houses in typically Karelian architecture. Two museums face the market square of the old town, one with historical collections and the other an art museum featuring the work of several art nouveau-era artists.

Albert Edelfeltin ateljeemuseo (Albert Edelfelt Studio Museum)

This is where the great man painted many of his most important works. Examples of his various periods are hung liberally all over the museum, and this is a must for art-lovers. ⓐ Edelfeltinpolku 3 ⓣ 019 577 414 ⓛ 10.00–16.00 Tues–Sun, June–Aug; 10.00–14.00 Tues–Sun, May & Sept. Admission charge

J L Runebergin koti (House of J L Runeberg)

Even before Sparr and Edelfelt made Porvoo into an art colony, it had been a centre of creative talent. Finland's national poet, Johan Ludvig Runeberg, lived and wrote here for more than two decades from 1852 onwards, drawing other talent of his times to Porvoo. The home has been a museum since 1882. ⓐ Aleksanterinkatu 3 ⓣ 019 581 330 ⓦ www.runeberg.net ⓛ 10.00–16.00 May–Aug; 10.00–16.00 Wed–Sun, Sept–Apr

Porvoon tuomiokirkko (Porvoo Cathedral)

Topping the hill is the cathedral, parts of which date from the 14th century, although it was largely reconstructed a century later and became a cathedral in 1723. Further reconstruction work had to be undertaken in 2006 after an arson attack damaged the roof, but the cathedral is now fully fixed and re-opened. Highlights are the ornate 1764 pulpit and wall paintings from the 15th century. ⓐ Kirkkotori 1 ⓣ 019 661 11 ⓛ 10.00–18.00 Mon–Fri, 10.00–14.00 Sat,

14.00–17.00 Sun, May–Sept; 10.00–14.00 Tues–Sat, 14.00–16.00 Sun, Oct–Apr

TAKING A BREAK

The following represent just a small selection from the wide choice of cafés and restaurants in Porvoo.

Café Fanny £ Friendly café in an 18th-century building on the Town Hall Square in old Porvoo, serving good coffee and freshly baked cinnamon buns. 🚋 Välikatu 13 ☎ 019 582 855 🕐 09.00–17.00 Apr & May; 09.00–18.00 Tues–Sun, June–Aug; 10.00–16.00 Tues–Sun, Sept–Mar

Old Town Café £ Sandwiches and pastries to eat in or take out. 🚋 Välikatu 1 ☎ 019 580 201 🌐 www.oldtown.fi 🕐 11.00–20.00 Mon–Thur, 10.00–22.00 Fri & Sat, 10.00–18.00 Sun, summer; 11.00–18.00 Mon–Thur, 11.00–20.00 Fri & Sat, winter

Porvoon Paahtimo ££ This red-tiled converted warehouse in the old historic centre of Porvoo is easy to spot. Excellent coffee choice and a river-facing terrace. 🚋 Mannerheiminkatu 2 ☎ 019 617 040 🌐 www.nexthotels.fi 🕐 12.00–23.00 Mon–Thur, 12.00–02.00 Fri, 10.00–02.00 Sat, 12.00–23.00 Sun

ACCOMMODATION

Hotel Seurahovi ££ Centrally located, the modern building offers nicely appointed rooms, saunas, a sports bar and restaurant. Close by, the 19th-century steam ship *Glückauf* is another dining choice. 🚋 Rauhankatu 27 ☎ 019 547 611 🌐 www.seurahovi.fi

Turku

Finland's oldest city at almost 800 years old, Turku was the capital until 1812. It is the most traditional medieval town in Finland, with a castle, marketplace, cathedral and a river harbour. In Turku you will see architecture ranging from the 1200s to art nouveau and the stunning modern Sibelius Museum by Woldemar Baeckman. Charming, if quiet, Turku proclaims itself as Finland's Christmas City. Visit then, or during the midsummer Medieval Festival, when the old square regains its medieval air, with craft stalls and food vendors. Turku has the distinction of being the European Capital of Culture in 2011.

Turku Touring Stop here for tourist information and maps of the southwest coast. ❷ Aurakatu 4 ❶ 02 262 7444 ❿ www.turkutouring.fi ❶ 09.00–17.00 Mon–Fri (also 10.00–16.00 Sat & Sun, Apr–Sept)

GETTING THERE

The easiest way to get to Turku is to take the hourly, quick Pendolino-train from Helsinki Railway Station (a journey of about two hours). Train travel in Finland is not cheap, but it is reliable, modern and comfortable. Although the train is the most popular method of travelling, you can also fly (❿ www.finnair.fi), or take a bus (❿ www.matkahuolto.fi).

SIGHTS & ATTRACTIONS

Forum Marinum

A combination of museum, shipyard and maritime research facility, the Forum includes two buildings (and 3,500 exhibits) and two historic vessels to tour, the full-rigger *Suomen Joutsen* and the minelayer *Keihässalmi*. Exhibits feature navy and commercial ships, local coastal

BOAT TRIPS

Opportunities to explore the River Aura and the archipelago include everything from a free ferry to dinner-dance cruises and day sails. The City Ferry (*Föri*) crosses the Aura from early morning until midnight, year round. From June to August the Pikkuföri river ferry plies the river from the Forum Marinum (€2.50). The **Ruissalo** (☎ 0400 509 523 ⓦ www.ruissalolautta.fi) cruises daily June–August between Turku and Ruissalo Island.

boats and culture. A second building contains boats and tools for boatbuilding. ⓐ Linnankatu 72 ☎ 02 282 9511 ⓦ www.forum-marinum.fi ⓛ 11.00–19.00 May–Sept; 10.00–18.00 Tues–Sun, Oct–Apr. Ships: 11.00–19.00 June–Aug ⓝ Bus: 1. Admission charge

Kuralan kylämäki (Village of Living History)

A working 1950s farm on the eastern outskirts of city takes visitors back half a century to smell fresh goodies baking in the farmhouse kitchen and pet baby animals in the barns. Hands-on activities bring the farm to life for children, who can make a whistle from a willow stick or play shops using real items from the period. At weekends in December the farm is decorated for the holidays and hosts a craft market, with prices far below those of street markets. ⓐ Jaanintie 45 ☎ 02 262 0420 ⓛ 10.00–18.00 Tues–Sun, mid-May–early Sept ⓝ Bus: 28

Muumimaailma (Moomin World)

Finland's most famous cartoon characters, the Moomins, will please even children who did not grow up with their adventures. Moomins cavort in the story settings, such as Moominhouse, Moominpapa's Boat,

Hemulens House and the Witch's Labyrinth. At the Pancake Factory children make their own pancake and choose favourite toppings. ⓐ Naantali ☎ 02 511 1111 ⓦ www.muumimaailma.fi 🕙 10.00–18.00 mid-June–late Aug Ⓝ Bus: 11, 110, 111; special bus from Turku harbour. Admission charge.

The Old Great Square

The ensemble of old buildings near the river was the historic centre of power, both church and state, when Turku was the capital. Brinkkala mansion was the residence of the Russian Governor General, and the stables in its courtyard are now artisans' studios. The entire square becomes a marketplace before Christmas and during the Medieval Market in the beginning of July. ⓦ www.keskiaikaisetmarkkinat.fi

Turun linna (Turku Castle)

Built between 1280 and 1650, Finland's largest castle is a defensive pile with outer walls 3 m (10 ft) thick. Enter its maze of stairways and passages through a picturesque courtyard to find towers, banqueting halls and a chapel with medieval woodcarving. Historical exhibits highlight events, customs and dress. ⓐ Linnankatu 80 ☎ 02 262 0300 ⓔ maakuntamuseo@turku.fi 🕙 10.00–18.00 Tues–Sun, May–Sept, 10.00–18.00 Tues, Thur–Sun, 12.00–20.00 Wed, Oct–Apr Ⓝ Bus: 1. Admission charge

Turun tuomiokirkko (Turku Cathedral)

In 1229, the Pope ordered a church to be built here, and the cathedral remained Catholic until the mid-16th century, when it became Finland's Lutheran mother church. Burned or pillaged 30 times throughout its history, it has been rebuilt each time, and remains a landmark of Finnish architecture. Although its lines are familiar perpendicular Gothic, the interior is entirely plastered, without visible stonework. ⓐ Tuomiokirkkotori 20 ⓣ 02 261 7100 ⓛ 09.00–19.00 (until 20.00 summer)

CULTURE

Aboa Vetus & Ars Nova

Built around an excavated city block of medieval Turku, Aboa Vetus explores not only the history of the site, but the archaeology of its discovery and preservation. The foundations have been dug 7 m (22 ft) deep to disclose glimpses of the medieval town, where artefacts, the stones themselves and exquisite models combine to tell the story. Guided tours are in English, daily July–Aug at 11.30.

Above, in the same building, Ars Nova couldn't be in sharper contrast to the medieval world below. More than 500 works by major contemporary and 20th-century artists from Finland and elsewhere trace movements and styles in modern art. ⓐ Itäinen Rantakatu 4–6 ⓣ 02 2500 552 ⓦ www.aboavetusarsnova.fi ⓛ 11.00–19.00 late Mar–mid-Sept; 11.00–19.00 Tues–Sun, Jan–late Mar & mid-Sept–mid-Dec ⓝ Bus: 13, 30, 55. Admission charge

Luostarinmäen käsityöläismuseo (Luostarinmäki Handicrafts Museum)

An entire neighbourhood of 40 homes, the only ones saved from the fire that destroyed Turku in 1827, is preserved as a museum village, showing how ordinary people lived. Homes and workshops open onto little courtyards, surrounded by stables and small rooms built as families grew. About 30 artisans demonstrate period crafts, from wire weaving and printing to carving shaved-wood ornaments, and you can buy from them or from the shop (see page 136). ⓐ Luostarinmäki ⓣ 02 262 0350 ⓛ 10.00–18.00 Tues–Sun, May–Sept ⓝ Bus: 3, 12, 18, 30. Admission charge

● *The atrium of the Sibelius Museum doubles as a concert hall*

Sibelius-museo (Sibelius Museum)

See this for the building, even if Sibelius and music leave you cold. Built in 1968, it was Finland's first glass and concrete building, and the concrete simulates rough-cut wood, its organic sand colour enhanced by lighting. Museum exhibits include rare musical instruments, sheet music and memorabilia, with signage in English. The atrium is a beautiful setting for Wednesday evening concerts.

ⓐ Piispankatu 17 ⓣ 02 215 4494 ⓦ www.sibeliusmuseum.abo.fi

🕐 11.00–16.00 Tues–Sun, also 18.00–20.00 Wed 🚌 Bus: 4, 28, 30, 50, 51, 53, 54. Admission charge

RETAIL THERAPY

Kiosks in the central square sell fresh produce, sizzling sausages, flowers and crafts, changing with the seasons, from early morning until 18.00 Monday to Friday, until 14.00 on Saturday. Overlooking this is the large **Sokos department store** (🅰 Eerikinkatu 11 ☎ 010 765 020) and from the square's upper corner runs Kauppiaskatu, the main shopping street. Small shops are scattered through the central streets around the market square and two shopping centres – Hansa and Forum – are close by.

Antiikkiliike Wanha Elias Shop or browse for antique furniture and decorative pieces. 🅰 Eerikinkatu 29 ☎ 0400 846 817 🌐 www.antiikkiliikewanhaelias.fi 🕐 10.00–17.00 Mon–Fri, 10.00–14.00 Sat

Au-Holmberg Oy This provides a fascinating insight into a goldsmith's workshop and shop. 🅰 Itäinen Rantakatu 64 ☎ 02 2316419 🌐 www.au-holmberg.fi 🕐 10.00–16.30 Mon–Fri

Fatabur The museum shop at Turku Castle sells a well-chosen selection of tasteful gifts, including historic glassware and jewellery reproductions, as well as traditional crafts (see page 132 for contact details). 🕐 10.00–17.45 Tues–Sun, May–Sept; 10.00–17.45 Tues, Thur–Sun, 10.00–19.45 Wed, Oct–Apr

Föripuoti Traditional and contemporary Finnish crafts.

 Sairashuoneenkatu 1  02 233 1073  10.00–14.00 Mon–Fri, 10.00–17.30 Thur

Iittala Outlet Finnish design, from glassware and china to cooking pots, in a factory outlet store.  Hämeenkatu 6  020 439 3547  10.00–20.00 Mon–Fri 10.00–18.00 Sat

Partiovaruste Everything for the outdoors – fishing gear, all-weather clothes, boots – as well as everyday wear.  Läntinen Pitkäkatu 13  010 3970 510  09.30–19.00 Mon–Fri, 09.30–15.00 Sat

Piha-Puoti (Luostarinmäki Handicrafts Museum Shop) The products of these authentic workshops – candlesticks and wall hooks woven from wire, framed stained-glass panels, straw wreaths, round wooden boxes and birds made of shaved wood – are sold in the museum's shop (see page 133 for contact details).  10.00–17.45 Tues–Sun, May–Sept & Dec–early Jan

Turku Market Hall In a traditional indoor market atmosphere, 50 merchants offer speciality foods, produce and crafts.  Eerikinkatu 16  07.00–17.30 Mon–Fri, 07.00–15.00 Sat

TAKING A BREAK

Stop at the Market Square for sausages or other quick foods. You'll also find food stalls in the market hall and at the two big open-air markets that fill Old Great Square in December and July.

Koulu £ Set in a restored school (*Koulu* means 'school'), the brewery serves house beers and others, along with lunch and dinner.

🅐 Eerikinkatu 18 ☏ 02 274 5757 🌐 www.panimoravintolakoulu.fi
🕐 11.00–02.00 Sun–Thur, 11.00–03.00 Fri & Sat. Food served
11.00–00.00 Mon–Fri, 12.00–00.00 Sat

Puutorin Vessa £ Sometimes it helps if you don't speak Finnish,
especially when a pub's name translates to 'The Wood Market's
Toilet'. This one is in a much-converted WC, hence the name –
another example of the Finns' wicked sense of humour. Snack
food is available along with a good selection of beers. 🅐 Puutori
☏ 02 233 8123 🌐 www.puutorinvessa.fi 🕐 12.00–00.00

Caffe Panini £–££ Italian panini sandwiches, pasta, pizza, salads and
other light dishes, in the sophisticated setting of Casagrande House,
near the river. 🅐 Linnankatu 3 ☏ 02 251 5310 🕐 11.00–22.00 Mon–Fri,
12.00–22.00 Sat & Sun

Börs Café ££ Light meals in a bright window-surrounded café
just off the Market Square. 🅐 Sokos Hotel Hamburger Börs,
Kauppiaskatu 6 ☏ 02 337 381

Café Daphne ££ Stay in the maritime spirit at the Forum Marinum
with lunch at this cheery cafe-restaurant, which boasts a full-size
sailboat inside. 🅐 Linnankatu 72 ☏ 02 337 3800 🕐 11.00–15.00 Mon,
11.00–16.00 Tues–Fri, 12.00–16.00 Sat & Sun

Café Restaurant Aula ££ For a break to separate the two very different
worlds of medieval life and 21st-century art, stop for coffee at this tidy
little museum café. 🅐 Aboa Vetus & Ars Nova, Itäinen Rantakatu 4–6
☏ 02 279 4936 🕐 11.00–18.00 Apr–Sept; 11.00–18.00 Tues–Sun,
Oct–Mar

Cafeteria Domcafé ££ Tucked into the brick vaults below the Cathedral, this café serves excellent coffee and cakes from historic recipes. ❸ Entrance at the Cathedral steps ❶ 02 261 7310 ⏲ Daily in summer, first three weekends in December

AFTER DARK

Along with several outstanding restaurants well worth spending an evening in, Turku has a rich cultural scene, with theatres, two orchestras, jazz and rock bars. The Turku Music Festival and Rockfestival Ruisrock are among the oldest in Scandinavia.

RESTAURANTS

Pub Old Bank £ Everyone meets at this popular pub in an historic Jugendstil bank building, where they serve 150 different beers in an English-style bar atmosphere. The food is good, too. ❸ Aurakatu 3 ❿ www.oldbank.fi ❶ 02 274 5700 ⏲ 12.00–00.00 Mon & Sun, 12.00–02.00 Tues–Thur, 12.00–03.00 Fri & Sat

Pavilion Vaakahuone £–££ Go for the fish, go for the swing and Dixieland, go for the summer scene at the river. Choose from several menus all grouped around the same terrace – seafood, pizza, giant Bratwurst or a coffee shop. Live music every night. ❸ Linnankatu 38 ❶ 02 515 3300 ❿ www.vaakahuone.fi ⏲ Daylight hours May–Aug (which means most of the night)

Cindyn Salonki ££ Uncomplicated dishes, many based on local seafood, are served in a boat moored on the river. ❸ Itäinen Rantakatu ❶ 02 250 2300 ❿ www.cindy.fi ⏲ 11.00–23.00 Mon–Fri, 12.00–23.00 Sat, 13.00–21.00 Sun

Blanko ££–£££ In the vaults of an old building near the Aurasilta Bridge, Blanko serves fusion cuisine drawn from everything from tapas to sashimi. Creative dishes include chanterelle and pumpkin lasagna or beetroot risotto. ⓐ Aurakatu 1 ⓣ www.blanko.net ⓛ 11.00–late Mon–Fri, 12.00–late Sat & Sun

Enkeliravintola ££–£££ The name of this restaurant translates as 'angel restaurant' and the food is indeed heavenly. Begin with a cup of warming *glögi*, while you look around at the playful décor. Then order dishes based on creative interpretations of Finnish cuisine: game terrine with lingonberries, creamy soup of forest mushrooms, *pot-au-feu* of lightly smoked pork or vegetarian mushroom pie. ⓐ Kauppiaskatu 16 ⓣ 02 231 8088 ⓦ www.enkeliravintola.fi ⓛ 11.00–15.00 Mon, 11.00–22.00 Tues–Fri, 13.00–22.00 Sat & Sun

Linnankatu 3 ££–£££ The presentation is worthy of the outstanding cuisine and surroundings; seafood dishes are superb, and the pâté is memorable. ⓐ Linnankatu 3 A ⓣ 02 233 9279 ⓦ www.linnankatu3.fi ⓛ 11.00–00.00 Mon–Fri, 17.00–00.00 Sat

Rocca £££ Fresh local ingredients are brilliantly treated by famous Finnish chef Antti Vahtera in dishes such as roast goose over a savoury ragout of mixed beans, and desserts such as espresso crème brulée or gingerbread sorbet. ⓐ Läntinen Rantakatu 55 ⓣ 020 755 9988 ⓛ 17.00–00.00 Tues–Sat

BARS & CLUBS
Galax Sleek dance club and late-night restaurant, which hosts well-known Finnish performers. Minimum age is 24 at weekends. ⓐ Aurakatu 6 ⓣ 02 284 3300 ⓛ 21.00–02.00 Wed, 21.00–04.00 Thur–Sat

ACCOMMODATION

Best Western Hotel Seaport £ Located in a charming converted customs warehouse right in the dock area, this makes a good choice if you are cruising in or out of Turku on a Baltic ferry. The rooms are attractive and comfortable. ⓐ Matkustajasatama ① 02 283 3000 Ⓦ www.bestwestern.com

Ruissalo Spa Hotel £–££ Pamper youself at this elegant spa on Ruissalo Island. A large, modern resort, its rooms are smart and there are several restaurants. The sport and spa facilities are superb. It sits amidst walking, jogging and cycling trails and beaches and is close to an 18-hole golf course. ⓐ Ruissalon puistotie 640 ① 02 445 5100 Ⓦ www.ruissalospa.fi

Naantali Spa Resort ££–£££ Saunas and aromatic aquatherapy are only the beginning of the facilities offered at this state-of-the-art resort spa near Turku. From the huge indoor pool, dive under the glass wall and stare at the winter sky from a steaming outdoor pool. ⓐ Naantali ① 02 445 5100 Ⓦ www.naantalispa.fi

Sokos Hotel Hamburger Börs ££–£££ You could hardly find a hotel closer to the centre of activity in this handsome town than the 346 rooms overlooking Market Square. These are nicely appointed in modern Scandinavian style. There are three saunas, a pool and other leisure facilities for guests, as well as seven restaurants. ⓐ Kauppiaskatu 6 ① 02 337 381 Ⓦ www.sokoshotels.fi

---

● *Helsinki Railway Station has Eliel Saarinen's most famous interior*

PRACTICAL
information

Directory

GETTING THERE

Helsinki can be reached by direct daily flights from major European hubs. Its location on the Baltic makes ferries a popular method of transport from Stockholm and from ports in Estonia and Germany. Most of these ferries also carry cars, so Finland can be incorporated into a driving holiday.

By air

Finnair flies to Helsinki-Vantaa (see page 50) from many UK and European airports, including several daily flights from Heathrow and

● *Helsinki-Vantaa Airport is Finland's largest modern gateway*

some direct flights from Manchester. SAS, British Airways and Blue1 also have direct flights to Helsinki-Vantaa from Heathrow. EasyJet flies to Vantaa from Gatwick, while Ryanair flies from Stansted to Tampere (see page 50).

Finnair operates daily direct flights from JFK in New York and, in the summer, from Toronto. SAS flies from several US gateways, but always connecting through Stockholm or Copenhagen.

Blue1 Ⓦ www.blue1.com
British Airways Ⓦ www.britishairways.com
easyJet Ⓦ www.easyjet.com
Finnair Ⓦ www.finnair.com
Ryanair Ⓦ www. ryanair.com
SAS Ⓦ www.scandinavian.net

Many people are aware that air travel emits CO_2, which contributes to climate change. You may be interested in the possibility of lessening the environmental impact of your flight through the charity **Climate Care** (Ⓦ www.climatecare.org), which offsets your CO_2 by funding environmental projects around the world.

By rail

Train travel is possible as far as Stockholm, from which point you must take a ferry. The trip from London's St Pancras International to Stockholm takes just over 18 hours, by Eurostar to Brussels, with changes in Cologne, Hamburg and Copenhagen, and the trains boarding ferries for the water crossings. The monthly *Thomas Cook European Rail Timetable* has up-to-date schedules for European international and national train services. Travellers from outside Europe who plan to use trains should investigate the various multi-day and multi-country train passes offered by Rail Europe. Eurail Selectpass includes rail travel in all four

Scandinavian countries (or any combination of them) plus Germany, with even greater savings for two or more people travelling together.

Eurostar 🕿 (UK) 08705 186186 🔘 www.eurostar.com

Rail Europe 🔘 www.raileurope.co.uk

Thomas Cook European Rail Timetable 🕿 (UK) 01733 416477; (USA) 1 800 322 3834 🔘 www.thomascookpublishing.com

By road

Next to a lucky hit for a rock-bottom air fare, the cheapest way to Helsinki from the UK is by bus, again via Stockholm, about 35 hours from London's Victoria Coach Station via Eurolines. From Stockholm you must take a ferry to Finland.

Eurolines 🕿 08705 143219 🔘 www.gobycoach.com or 🔘 www.eurolines.com

Car trips to Finland from the UK must include at least one crossing by car ferry, which adds significantly to the cost. But this remains a budget-friendly option if several people are travelling together. The shortest route, the Via Baltica, is to Tallinn, Estonia, making the final short crossing on one of the several daily car ferries to Helsinki.

Cars in Finland drive on the right-hand side of the road. For rules, speed limits and safety tips for drivers, see page 51.

By water

Sweden, Germany and Estonia are all connected to Finland by ferry links. Tallink Silja operates a useful service from Rostock in Germany to Helsinki four days a week, with the journey taking around 26 hours. The same company has around seven departures every day to Helsinki from Tallinn, Estonia (two hours) and nightly departures from Stockholm, Sweden. Viking Line operates both day and night journeys between Stockholm and Helsinki, as well as two departures per day from Tallinn to Helsinki.

Tallink Silja Ⓦ www.tallinksilja.com

Viking Ⓦ www.vikingline.fi

ENTRY FORMALITIES

Citizens of the UK, Republic of Ireland, USA, Canada and Australia need only a valid passport to enter Finland and do not require visas. Citizens of EU countries other than the UK need only a valid national identity card, or a passport. Citizens of South Africa must have a passport and visa to enter. Visa forms can be obtained from your nearest Finnish embassy or consulate.

EU citizens can bring goods for personal use when arriving from another EU country, but must observe the limits on tobacco (800 cigarettes) and spirits (ten litres of alcohol over 22 per cent proof, 20 litres of wine). Limits for non-EU nationals are 200 cigarettes and one litre of spirits, two litres of wine.

MONEY

The currency in Finland is the euro (€), which is divided into 100 cents. Notes are in €5, 10, 20, 50, 100, 200 and 500 denominations and coins are €1 and €2, plus 5, 10, 20 and 50 cents. 1- and 2-cent coins are not used in Finland, and prices in shops are generally rounded to the nearest 5 cents. The best means of obtaining local currency is by using a debit card. Although many banks charge a fee for this, these are usually less than cash advances on credit cards, and are at a more favourable exchange rate than cash transactions or travellers' cheques. ATMs (cashpoints) can be found nearly everywhere, easily recognised by yellow hoods. Finns call an ATM an *otto*.

Credit cards are very widely used in Helsinki, even by taxis, and you can often pay by credit card in pubs and get cash back if you're short. Travellers' cheques can be cashed at banks, post offices and in most hotels, and are widely accepted in major shops and stores in Helsinki.

Bureaux de change can be found in airports and near the railway station. You can also change money at Helsinki's large bank **Nordea** (Main branch: ⓐ Aleksanterinkatu 52 ⓘ 02 003 000 ⓒ 09.30–16.15 Mon–Fri).

◗ *Gigantic art nouveau guardians of Helsinki Railway Station*

HEALTH, SAFETY & CRIME

Finnish medical care is excellent, with English-speaking doctors and modern clinics and hospitals. Free emergency services are available to all visitors. Citizens from the European Union (and a few other European countries) can also claim free treatment for more minor complaints on production of a European Health Insurance Card (EHIC). All visitors, but particularly those without an EHIC, are advised to take out adequate travel insurance.

If you are there in the winter and take part in winter sports, remember that the thickness of ice on lakes and bays is hard to judge.

Skate or walk on ice only with a trained guide or where a number of others are also on the ice. Never venture onto ice alone, even if you think you are sure of its strength.

Finland is one of the safest countries in the world in which to travel, but remember that wherever tourists gather, there will be occasional pickpockets. Lock valuables in the hotel safe or leave them at home. You are not likely to need your diamond tiara in Helsinki.

OPENING HOURS

Most shops are open from 09.00 to between 16.00 and 18.00 on Monday to Friday, and from 09.00 to between 14.00 and 16.00 on Saturday. Shops are not open on Sundays except in the summer and the run-up to Christmas.

TOILETS

Public facilities are common in Helsinki, but they may not be open all hours. Those inside buildings such as the public markets close with the market. Those in parks may be open limited hours and closed Sunday and in the winter. Those in hotels and cafés are a good alternative when others are closed.

CHILDREN

Finns are fond of children and frequently take their own out and about, so most hotels and restaurants are prepared. Those with music and entertainment, as well as other nightspots, do not welcome children, any more than their equivalents would in any city. However, Helsinki has plenty of family-friendly attractions.

Korkeasaari Zoo (see page 109) is worthwhile for the entire family, with rare cats (including snow leopards), red pandas, a specialist collection of animals indigenous to the Arctic and, by contrast, many Amazonian species in the Amazonia micro-climate house. The trip there by ferry is fun for children, too.

For the underwater 'zoo' experience, you can take them to Sea Life Helsinki (see page 90), which explores marine life while offering aquatic adventures. Nearby is Linnanmäki Amusement Park (see page 88), the perfect place to keep kids amused all day with rides, a monorail, an open-air theatre, eating places that welcome children and a free playground. And to make you feel good about every euro you spend on rides, all the income goes to the national child welfare organisations that run the park.

It's almost guaranteed that you'll enjoy playing at the Helsinki Playground (see page 66) just as much as the kids do. Plenty of access to all the hands-on activities is assured by timed ticketing. Choose your two-hour time slot, at 10.00, 12.00, 14.00, 16.00 or 18.00.

The **Serena Waterpark** (📍 Tornimaentie 10, Espoo ☎ 09 887 0550 🌐 www.serena.fi 🕐 11.00–20.00 🚍 Bus: 339. Admission charge) is a bit out of town, but reachable by bus from the central bus station in Helsinki. This is a good diversion if the weather turns hot in the summer, or when you need a breath of the tropics on a wintry day. Children won't believe that a water park stays open in the winter. It's a low-key splash park, but good for young children. Another good option for watery activities is the **Flamingo Spa** (📍 Tasetie 8 ☎ 020 7785 201 🌐 www.flamingospa.fi 🕐 Complex open 24 hrs; opening hours for individual attractions vary), a new spa, water park and entertainment centre near the airport. Here you'll find some excellent attractions for adults as well as for children.

Performances for children are staged on Suomenlinna Island during the summer, with a variety of shows and theatre companies participating. The Helsinki City Tourist & Convention Bureau (see page 153) will have schedules. Older children will enjoy exploring the fortress and, as with the zoo, the boat ride there is an adventure itself. They will also enjoy the hands-on activities at Seurasaari Open-air Museum, as well as the unusual old buildings.

COMMUNICATIONS
Internet

Public internet access is widely available in Helsinki as well as in larger towns, with plenty of internet cafés and public libraries offering access. Many hotels have a computer or broadband connection available for guests.

TELEPHONING HELSINKI

The country code for Finland is 358. The city code for Helsinki is 09, for Turku 02, for Porvoo 019. To call from outside Finland, dial the international access code of the country you're calling from (00 from the UK, 001 from the US), then 358, then the Finnish city code (omitting the first 0), and finally the local number you require. From inside Finland, dial the city code and number. Note that there is no set length for local Finnish telephone numbers.

TELEPHONING ABROAD

To make an international call from Finland, dial 00, then the country code (UK 44, Republic of Ireland 353, USA and Canada 1, Australia 61, New Zealand 64, South Africa 27) and the area code (omitting the initial zero in UK area codes) and then the number you require.

A reliable internet café in the centre is **Waynes Coffee**
(ⓐ Kaisaniemenkatu 3 ☎ 040 413 9401 🕐 08.00–21.00 Mon–Fri,
10.00–21.00 Sat, 12.00–21.00 Sun). If you want to read your emails
and have a good night out at the same time, try **Mbar** (ⓐ Lasipalatsi/
Mannerheimintie 22–24 ☎ 09 6124 5420 🌐 www.mbar.fi 🕐 09.00–
00.00 Mon & Tues, 09.00–02.00 Wed & Thur, 09.00–03.00 Fri & Sat,
12.00–00.00 Sun), which offers computers and a WLAN connection
for customers as well as DJs every night.

Phone
Due in part to extremely high levels of mobile phone usage in
Finland, public telephones are not used. Your best option is to buy a
pre-paid Finnish SIM card for your own mobile. Before making a call
from your hotel room, check the rates: they are often extortionate.

Post
Finnish post is not only prompt, it is safe; the Finns are honest to
their toes, so what you mail will arrive safely and quickly. Helsinki's
main post office is **Posti Central Office** (ⓐ Elielinaukio 2 ☎ 0200 71000
🕐 07.00–21.00 Mon–Fri, 10.00–18.00 Sat & Sun). A postcard should
arrive at EU destinations within three to four days and will take
around a week to reach North America.

ELECTRICITY
Current in Finland is 220V AC, at 50 Hz. Australian, New Zealand,
US, Canadian and some South African and UK appliances will need
adapters to fit Finnish wall outlets. If you are travelling in other
Scandinavian countries, note that outlets are not all the same.
Appliances using only 110V will need transformers, as well as
plug adapters.

MEDIA

Helsinki's newspaper *Helsingin Sanomat* publishes an English-language version, good for local news and events. International newspapers are available at news-stands and in hotels. For information on current events, contact the tourist office or consult the brochures and magazines listed on page 32.

△ *Ferries drop their passengers right into the very heart of Helsinki*

TRAVELLERS WITH DISABILITIES

Lifts provide access to all floors (including the subterranean tunnels that connect much of the central area) in the major department stores and shopping centres, as well as the railway station and Kinopalatsi Cinema Centre. When using the tunnels, you can access street level through these buildings or by a number of lifts throughout the system. The zoo, Suomenlinna Fortress, the Ateneum and a number of other tourist sights have disabled access to most of their facilities, as do the Opera House and Finlandia Hall. The outdoor areas of Seurasaari Open-air Museum are accessible, but the historic buildings are not.

There is normally space in Finnish trains for wheelchairs, as well as special tables, allowing for wheelchair manoeuvres. These spaces need reservations, but there is normally no extra charge.

For specially equipped taxis, call one of the following:

Helsingin Palveluauto Oy ⓐ Helsingin Palveluauto ⓣ 020 743 2150
Invataxi Iiro's Taxi Service ⓣ 040 500 6070

TOURIST INFORMATION

Helsinki City Tourist & Convention Bureau ⓐ Pohjoisesplanadi 19, Helsinki ⓣ 09 3101 3300 ⓦ www.visithelsinki.fi ⓛ 09.00–20.00 Mon–Fri, 09.00–18.00 Sat & Sun, May–Sept; 09.00–18.00 Mon–Fri, 10.00–16.00 Sat & Sun, Oct–Apr

Visitors from the UK can contact the London branch of the **Finnish Tourist Board** (ⓐ 177–179 Hammersmith Road, London W6 8BS ⓣ 020 8600 7283 ⓦ www.visitfinland.com).

Emergencies

Police, ambulance or fire emergency number ❶ 112

MEDICAL SERVICES

Should you become ill in Finland, you have several sources of information on English-speaking doctors – although you will find that most speak rather good English. The consular office of your embassy can provide a list. You can also go prepared with the appropriate pages from the directory published by the International Association of Medical Assistance for Travellers (IAMAT), a non-profit organisation that provides information on health-related travel issues all over the world, as well as lists of English speaking doctors Ⓦ www.iamat.org

24-hour medical and dental treatment can be obtained at:
Hospital Mehiläinen ❸ Pohjoinen Hesperiankatu 17 ❶ 010 414 0444

POLICE

For non-urgent police assistance, visit the **main police station**

EMERGENCY PHRASES

Help!	**Help me, please!**
Apua!	Voitko auttaa!
Erpuer!	*Voytko owttah!*

Call an ambulance/Call a doctor/Call the police!
Soittakaaa ambulanssi/Kutsukaa lääkäri/Soittakaaa poliisi!
Soi-terkah ermbulernsi/Kutsukah lahkari/Soi-terkah polleesi!

(🅐 Punanotkonkatu 2 ☎ 071 877 0111). There is a more central precinct at 🅐 Pieni Roobertinkatu 1–3 ☎ 09 1891.

Lost property
Police Lost Property Office 🅐 Punanotkonkatu 2 ☎ 071 877 3180
🕙 08.00–16.15 Mon–Fri (enquiries by phone 10.00–14.00 Mon–Fri)
🚊 Tram: 10
Transport Lost Property For items lost on trains, buses, trams and at the airport. You can make enquiries by telephone. 🅐 Mäkelänkatu 56
☎ 0600 410 06 🌐 www.loytotavara.net 🕙 09.00–18.00 Mon–Fri

EMBASSIES & CONSULATES
Consulates and consular sections of embassies handle emergencies of travelling citizens. After reporting it to the police, your consulate or embassy should be the first place you turn to if a passport is lost or stolen.
British Embassy 🅐 Itäinen puistotie 17 ☎ 09 228 65100
🌐 http://ukinfinland.fco.gov.uk 🕙 08.30–15.00 Mon–Fri,
late June–late Aug; 09.00–17.00 rest of year
Canadian Embassy 🅐 Pohjoisesplanadi 25 B ☎ 09 228 530
🌐 www.canada.fi
Irish Embassy 🅐 Erottajankatu 7 A ☎ 09 646 006
New Zealand Consulate 🅐 Kohdematkat Oy, Hietalahdenranta 13
☎ 02 470 1818
South African Embassy 🅐 Rahapajankatu 1 A 5 (3rd Floor)
☎ 09 6860 3100 🌐 www.southafricanembassy.fi 🕙 Consular
hours 09.00–14.00 Mon–Fri
United States Embassy, Consular Office 🅐 Itäinen puistotie 14 B
☎ 09 616 250 🌐 www.usembassy.fi 🕙 09.00–12.00 Mon–Thur;
phone hours: 14.00–16.00 Mon–Thur

A

Aboa Vetus 133
accommodation 36–41
  Porvoo 129
  Turku 140
air travel 50, 59–60, 142–3
Albert Edelfelt Studio
  Museum 128
Amos Anderson
  Art Museum 71
Arabia Museum 111–12
architecture & design
  14–15, 20–2, 62, 64–5,
  72, 112–14
Ars Nova 133
art nouveau 14–15, 17,
  64–5, 66, 67–8, 72,
  112–14
Ateneum 71

B

bars & clubs see nightlife
beaches 35, 110, 111
boat travel 54, 58, 106–8,
  124, 131, 142, 144–5
Botanical Gardens 67
bus travel 51, 58–60,
  124, 144

C

Cable Factory 94
cafés
  Esplanadi &
    Harbour 80–3
  Islands &
    outskirts 118–20
  Porvoo 129
  Turku 136–8
  Western & northern
    Helsinki 99–101
car hire 60
children 148–50
Christmas markets 13, 76–7

Church in the Rock 91–2
cinemas 31–2, 85, 105
climate 8
crime 148
cruises see boat travel
culture 20–2
customs & duty 145
cycling 59

D

Dance Theatre
  Hurjaruuth 94
design see architecture
  & design
Design District 20, 62
Design Museum 72
Didrichsen Art Museum 112
disabled travellers 153
Doll & Toy Museum 113
driving 51–4, 60, 124, 144

E

Ehrensvärd Museum 113
electricity 151
embassies &
  consulates 155
emergencies 154–5
entertainment 30–2
  see also nightlife
Esplanadi 64–5
events & festivals 9–13,
  46–7

F

ferries see boat travel
Finlandia Hall 73
Finnish Museum
  of Photography 94
Flamingo Spa 149
food & drink 26–9
Forum Marinum 130–1

G

Gallen-Kallela
  Museum 112

H

health 147–8, 154
Helsinki Car Museum 95
Helsinki Card 58
Helsinki City Art
  Museum 95
Helsinki Contemporary
  Dance Theatre 74
Helsinki Music Centre 73
Helsinki Playground 66
Helsinki Railway
  Station 50–1, 66
Hietaniemi Cemetery 86
history 16–17
Hotel and Restaurant
  Museum 94
hotels
  see accommodation
House of J L Runeberg 128
Hvitträsk 112–14

I

internet 150–1

J

Jugend Hall 66
Jugendstil
  see art nouveau

K

Kaisaniemi Botanical
  Gardens 67
Kallio Church 67
Katajanokka 67–8
Kauppatori 68
Kekkonen Museum 114–15
Kiasma Museum of
  Contemporary Art 74
Korkeasaari Zoo 109–10,
  148–9
Kunsthalle 96

L

language 22, 25, 29, 55,
  154, 160

lifestyle 18–19
Linnanmäki Amusement
   Park 88, 149
listings 22, 32, 152
lost property 155
Luostarinmäki Handicrafts
   Museum 133
Lutheran Cathedral,
   Helsinki 70

M
Market Square 68
media 152
money 145–6
Moomin World 131–2
Museum of Cultures 95
Museum of Finnish
   Architecture 75

N
National Museum
   of Finland 74–5
National Opera 75
National Romantics
   14–15, 112–14
National Theatre 75
nightlife 30–2
   Esplanadi &
      Harbour 84–5
   Turku 138–9
   Western & northern
      Helsinki 103–5

O
Old Great Square,
   Turku 132
Olympic Stadium 88–90
opening hours 148

P
Parliament House 55
passports & visas 145
phone 150–1
Pihlajasaari Island 110

Pohjola Insurance
   Building 68
police 154–5
Porvoo 124–9
Porvoo Cathedral 128–9
post 151
public holidays 13
public transport 58–60

R
rail travel 50–1, 59–60,
   66, 143–4
restaurants 26–9
   Esplanadi &
      Harbour 83–4
   Islands &
      outskirts 120–2
   Turku 138–9
   Western & northern
      Helsinki 101–3

S
safety 147–8
saunas 19, 35
Sea Life Helsinki 90–1, 149
seasons 8
Sederholm House 74
Senaatintori 70
Senate Square 70
Serena Waterpark 149
Seurasaari Open-air
   Museum 114
shopping 24–5, 48–9
   Esplanadi &
      Harbour 76–80
   Islands &
      outskirts 115–17
   Turku 135–6
   Western & northern
      Helsinki 96–9
Sibelius Monument 91
Sibelius Museum,
   Turku 134–5

Sinebrychoff Art
   Museum 95–6
smoking 29
sport & relaxation 34–5
Summer Theatre,
   islands 114
Suomenlinna
   Fortress 110–11
swimming 35

T
taxis 58–9
Temppeliaukio
   Church 91–2
Theatre Museum 94
time difference 50
tipping 29
toilets 148
tourist information 153
tram travel 58
Tropicario 70
Turku 130–40
Turku Castle 132
Turku Cathedral 132–3

U
Uspenski Cathedral 70–1
Uunisaari Island 111

V
Vesikko 113
Village of Living
   History 131

W
weather 8, 48–9
Winter Garden 88
winter sports 34–5

Z
Zodiak Centre for
   New Dance 94
zoo 109–10, 148–9

Editorial/project management: Lisa Plumridge
Copy editor: Monica Guy
Layout/DTP: Alison Rayner

The publishers would like to thank the following companies
and individuals for supplying their copyright photographs for this
book: A1 Pix, pages 33, 108–9 & 152; Dainis Derics/iStockphoto.com,
page 18; Finnish Tourist Board, pages 27, 34, 46, 89 & 142; Olli Laine/
iStockphoto.com, page 11; Tero Puha, pages 7, 21, 39, 42–3, 59, 61,
100 & 116; Rūta Saulytė-Laurinavičienė/Dreamstime.com, page 5;
Stillman Rogers Photography, pages 8, 15, 17, 49, 69, 72–3, 78, 82,
90, 92–3, 116, 123, 125, 134, 141 & 146–7.

Send your thoughts to
books@thomascook.com

- **Found a great bar, club, shop or must-see sight that we don't feature?**
- **Like to tip us off about any information that needs a little updating?**
- **Want to tell us what you love about this handy little guidebook and more importantly how we can make it even handier?**

Then here's your chance to tell all! Send us ideas, discoveries and recommendations today and then look out for your valuable input in the next edition of this title.

Email the above address (stating the title) or write to:
pocket guides Series Editor, Thomas Cook Publishing, PO Box 227,
Coningsby Road, Peterborough PE3 8SB, UK.

WHAT'S IN YOUR GUIDEBOOK?

Independent authors Impartial up-to-date information from our travel experts who meticulously source local knowledge.

Experience Thomas Cook's 165 years in the travel industry and guidebook publishing enriches every word with expertise you can trust.

Travel know-how Thomas Cook has thousands of staff working around the globe, all living and breathing travel.

Editors Travel-publishing professionals, pulling everything together to craft a perfect blend of words, pictures, maps and design.

You, the traveller We deliver a practical, no-nonsense approach to information, geared to how you really use it.

Useful phrases

English	Finnish	Approx pronunciation
BASICS		
Yes	Joo	*Yoo*
No	Ei	*Aye*
Please	Kiitos/Ole hyvä	*Keetoss/Oleh hewva*
Thank you	Kiitos	*Keetoss*
Hello	Hei	*Hey*
Goodbye	Näkemiin	*Nakehmeen*
Excuse me	Anteeksi	*Erntehksi*
Sorry	Sori	*Sorry*
That's okay	Ole hyvä	*Oleh hewva*
I don't speak Finnish	En puhu suomea	*En puhu suormeah*
Do you speak English?	Puhutko englantia?	*Puhutko ehnglerntier?*
Good morning	Hyvää huomenta	*Hewwa-a huomehnter*
Good afternoon	Hyvää päivää	*Hewwa-a pa-i-va-a*
Good evening	Hyvää iltaa	*Hewwa-a iltah*
Goodnight	Hyvää yötä	*Hewwa-a ew-erta*
My name is ...	Minun nimeni on ...	*Minun nimehni on ...*
NUMBERS		
One	Yksi	*Ewksi*
Two	Kaksi	*Kerksi*
Three	Kolme	*Kolmeh*
Four	Neljä	*Nehlyah*
Five	Viisi	*Veesi*
Six	Kuusi	*Koosi*
Seven	Seitsemän	*Sehtsehman*
Eight	Kahdeksan	*Kerdehksern*
Nine	Yhdeksän	*Ewkh-dehksan*
Ten	Kymmenen	*Kewmehnehn*
Twenty	Kaksikymmentä	*Kerksikewmehnta*
Fifty	Viisikymmentä	*Veesikewmehnta*
One hundred	Sata	*Ser-ter*
SIGNS & NOTICES		
Airport	Lentokenttä	*Lenthokenthae*
Railway station	Rautatieasema	*Rawtahtie-ah-sehmah*
Platform	Laituri	*Laytuhri*
Smoking/Non-smoking	Tupakointi/ Tupakointi kielletty	*Tupahkhointi/* *Tuphahkhointi kie-lettue*
Toilets	WC/Vessa	*Veesee/Vessah*
Ladies/Gentlemen	Naiset/Miehet	*Naihset/Miehet*
Metro/tram/bus	Metro/raitiovaunu/bussi	*Metro/rayti-o-vawnu/bussi*